LYNNE MCGEACHIE's interest in Beatrix Potter began many years ago. The discovery of Potter's Perthshire connections and the fact that *The Tale of Peter Rabbit* had its beginnings there inspired Lynne to write *The Tale o Peter Kinnen*, the first translation into Scots of that classic of children's literature.

Lynne has been climbing and exploring the hills of her native Scotland for decades, delighting in the landscapes, wildlife and history of her beautiful and fascinating homeland. In 1991 she and her husband, with whom she shares her love of the hills and wild places, completed the Munros.

BEATRIX POTTER'S SCOTLAND

Her Perthshire Inspiration

LYNNE McGEACHIE

Luath Press Limited
EDINBURGH
www.luath.co.uk

First published 2010

ISBN: 978-1-906817-43-5

The paper used in this book is recyclable. It is made from low chlorine pulps
produced in a low energy, low emissions manner from renewable forests.

Printed and bound by
Bell & Bain Ltd., Glasgow

Typeset in 9.5 Quadraat by
3btype.com

CONTENTS

FOREWORD

BEATRIX POTTER IS NEARLY always associated solely with the Lake District. Many of her much-loved 'little books' are, indeed, set there and her farming activities and acquisition of farms and property there have resulted, through the generosity of her bequests to The National Trust, in our ability to have access to and enjoy so much of the Lake District today. But what is not widely known is that Beatrix's love and appreciation of nature was nurtured in Scotland, that *The Tale of Peter Rabbit* and *The Tale of Mr. Jeremy Fisher* were both written there and that Beatrix Potter's association with Scotland played an important part in her life.

When Margaret Lane surprised the world in 1946 with her biography, *The Tale of Beatrix Potter*, she revealed that there was a great deal more to Miss Potter than anyone knew, but in her book there is scarce mention of Scotland. It was not until 12 years later, on the evening of Easter Monday, 1958, that the renowned Potter scholar, Leslie Linder, finally cracked the code in which Beatrix had written her teenage journal – and the importance that Scotland had played in Beatrix's life began to emerge. It would be another eight years before *The Journal of Beatrix Potter* was published and only then was Beatrix's fascinating record of her regular visits to Scotland available for all to share.

Now Lynne McGeachie tells in full the story of Beatrix Potter's Scottish connections: the influence of her Scottish nurse; Beatrix's delight in the family holidays taken there; her sharing of knowledge about fungi with the postman and renowned mycologist, Charlie McIntosh, and the origin of the first of her books through her picture letters. Lynne McGeachie combines her knowledge of the history and geography of Scotland with Beatrix Potter's accounts of her visits there. It makes a fascinating – and revealing – story.

Judy Taylor, MBE

LIST OF ILLUSTRATIONS

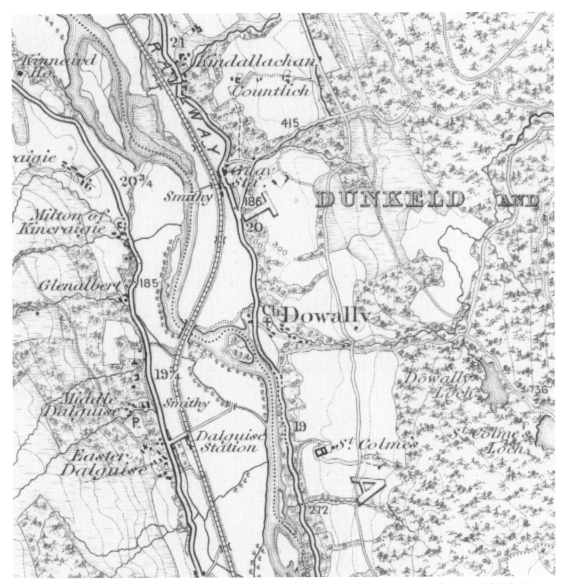

Map of Dalguise showing the area as Beatrix would have known it. Dalguise House is midway between Glenalbert and Middle Dalguise.
One inch to the mile maps of Scotland, **2nd edition. Sheet 55 Blair Atholl. Surveyed 1895, published 1897.**

Reproduced by kind permission of the National Library of Scotland

ACKNOWLEDGEMENTS

IT IS WITH PLEASURE that I express my sincere gratitude to a number of people who have helped and encouraged me in the writing of this book.

Judy Taylor MBE, author of many books about Beatrix Potter and an authority on her, read the manuscript and made numerous valuable suggestions. In addition, Judy patiently answered my many questions and queries and provided much important advice and guidance for which I am enormously grateful. She also graciously wrote the Foreword.

I am also indebted to Irene Whalley for her insightful comments and for generously sharing her scholarly knowledge of Potter with me.

To Enid Bassom I extend my thanks. Her eye for detail was most welcome.

As well as taking an enthusiastic interest in the book the Committee of The Beatrix Potter Society gave generous permission to reproduce photographs, taken by Rupert Potter, from their Collection and special thanks go to Jenny Akester for kindly supplying these on disc. In addition the Committee gave permission to quote extracts from two of their publications, Peter Rabbit's Other Tale and The Tale o Peter Kinnen.

The publisher Frederick Warne & Co. kindly gave permission to quote extensively from The Journal of Beatrix Potter and other sources. They also gave valued permission to reproduce several illustrations by Beatrix Potter, a photograph taken by Rupert Potter and one by A. F. Mackenzie. In this respect my sincere thanks to Nicola Saunders, Licensing Director, Frederick Warne.

Other quotations by Beatrix Potter in the Introduction and in Chapters One, Three and Four are from books published by The Horn Book, Inc. and these are gratefully acknowledged.

The two fungi paintings by Beatrix Potter and the photograph of Charles McIntosh are reproduced by kind permission of Perth Museum and Art Gallery, Perth and Kinross Council, Scotland.

My ancestors and grandparents were Perthshire folk, deep-rooted there, as is my mother. Their love of that fine countryside has quietly passed through successive generations to me and perhaps enabled me, therefore, to better understand Beatrix Potter's Perthshire.

In connection with this book I remember Mist, our beautiful Border Collie, who faithfully kept me company throughout the writing of it no matter how late the hour.

Finally and above all my love and thanks to my husband, Gibson. His help and advice in so many ways has made the book possible.

Any errors or omissions are of course mine.

Lynne McGeachie

'...so I shall tell you a story...'[1]

THE NAME OF BEATRIX POTTER, author and illustrator of the world-famous 'Peter Rabbit' books is almost always associated with the English Lake District.

It was, however, somewhere else that first influenced Beatrix and inspired her imagination long before she went to the Lake District. This special place was the beautiful countryside of Perthshire in Scotland.

For many years of her childhood Beatrix spent idyllic holidays there. It became her paradise on earth. Her affinity with Perthshire and especially the area around the tiny hamlet of Dalguise, and nearby the peaceful countryside surrounding the ancient burgh of Dunkeld, provided the foundation for Beatrix Potter's instinctive creative brilliance.

This eventually revealed itself in the pages of the little books that made her famous. Characters such as Mrs Tiggy-winkle and Mr Jeremy Fisher, beloved by generations of children, had their beginnings in Beatrix Potter's Perthshire. And it was in Perthshire too that the story of Peter Rabbit was first told.

INTRODUCTION

THE JOURNEY NORTH FROM the Fair City of Perth to Inverness the Highland Capital by way of Dunkeld, Blair Atholl and the Pass of Drumochter, is one that has been made by countless travellers for centuries. The valley of the River Tay is a green and pleasant land, fringed by beautiful wooded slopes, patched by broad farmlands and scattered small communities. There is an air of quiet continuity. The clear, salmon haunted waters of the River Tay pass the graceful arches of Thomas Telford's fine bridge at Dunkeld. From this historic little town the road continues northward through an ancient landscape towards high moors brown and purple in the distance, and to blue hills beyond.

Today the journey from Perth to Inverness by car or by train, unless delayed by snow, is quick and easy. Yet the same hills and the mighty River Tay steadfastly continue to dwarf centuries and all who peopled them. Of those who came this way through Perthshire, and they were many and varied, the earliest travellers were prehistoric people who left their enigmatic traces in stone circles and gaunt standing stones, silent witness to Roman legion and Viking raider. Faint echoes may yet be discerned of others too, Jacobites and King's men, monks, fugitives, artisans, paupers, poets and artists, road builders and generals. All crossed the highland line on foot or, if they were lucky enough, on horseback. Of these early travellers few would have had the leisure, or for that matter the inclination to lift their eyes to the beauty of the natural scene around them. That luxury came later to others who had.

One such gentleman was Rupert Potter of London. It was the custom for wealthy families to leave London in the summer months and accordingly, in 1871, Mr Potter rented Dalguise House for himself, his wife Helen and their little daughter Beatrix. Such a spacious Perthshire residence amidst its own well-kept grounds, and a convenient carriage drive from Dunkeld, seemed to Mr Potter the ideal holiday location for a summer of leisure and fishing. Such activities would also prove irresistible to friends he invited to join the family at various points during their three month long sojourn in the Highlands. This was the era of great railway developments, of which the Potters made full use, taking with them by train from London to Dalguise and later Birnam, their own carriage and horses and of course their own servants and coachman. Rupert and Helen Potter had no intention of leaving to chance any of their accustomed routines or home comforts.

For the Potter children, Beatrix and later her brother Bertram, coming to beautiful Perthshire from their home in grey London was a revelation. Dalguise became the family's summer holiday destination for 11 successive summers until 1881, when it was no longer available. For Beatrix, then aged five, Dalguise and the surrounding Perthshire countryside became the centre of her happiest childhood memories, enduring into old age. She fell in love with its inspiring beauty and with its peacefulness. At the age of 70 she wrote, '...it sometimes happens that the town child is more alive to the fresh beauty of the country than a child who is country born... My brother and I were born in London... But our descent – our interests and our joy was in the north country.'[1]

CHAPTER ONE

'The spirit of enquiry leads up a lane
which hath no ending.' [1]

HELEN BEATRIX POTTER was born on 28 July 1866 at No 2 Bolton Gardens, Kensington, London, and she grew up there. She was the first child of Rupert and Helen Potter but to avoid being confused with her mother she was known by her second name, Beatrix, and simply as B to her parents and family friends. Bolton Gardens was not a home she remembered with any great affection, a fact she recalled wryly almost a lifetime later, with the comment 'my unloved birthplace'[2], when she learned that the house had been destroyed in 1940 by German bombs.

Her parents were rich. Their wealth had been generated through the hard work of their vigorous predecessors. Consequently Rupert and Helen Potter had each inherited Lancashire cotton fortunes and considered themselves members of the professional upper middle-classes. Rupert Potter was a barrister-at-law. He had been called to the Bar in 1857 and established his chambers in London at Lincoln's Inn. He rather liked the notion of being a barrister-at-law and the respect and dignity associated with that profession. In 1860 he moved his chambers to New Square and for the next 30 years others conducted business from there on his behalf, for there is no evidence that he ever practised. He did not need to. He was wealthy and much preferred to be a gentleman of leisure, a style admirably fitted to his self-image. Now far removed from any association with 'grubby moneymaking', the Potters led lives of leisured gentility, pursuing their own interests from the comfort of their London home. It was however a formal, strictly ordered life of Victorian respectability they chose to impose upon themselves and all in their household. Any display of showiness or vibrancy, the latter characteristic a distinct hallmark of their parents and ancestors, was simply out of the question as far as the Potters of No 2 Bolton Gardens were concerned.

Nevertheless Rupert Potter was proud of his father. Edmund Potter was a self-made man from a modest Manchester background, who valued education as a means of getting on in life. In keeping with the cherished belief held by the Victorians that anything was possible through hard work and application, Edmund Potter somehow managed to get enough precious education to take him forward into the calico-printing trade. A handsome, enlightened man of gentle disposition, in 1829 he had married the beautiful and intelligent Jessie

Crompton. Edmund was rewarded for his skill and integrity by becoming the owner of Dinting Vale Works at Glossop near Manchester, as well as a magistrate and eventually Liberal Member of Parliament for Carlisle. He believed in education, religious tolerance and equality and encouraged others, regardless of background, to seek to better themselves, which he declared would in turn lead to wider horizons. He was a humane figure interested in every aspect of life, yet through no fault of his own suffered the cruel blow of bankruptcy when the world market in calico-printing changed and his firm collapsed. It says much for the remarkable person Edmund Potter was that he started all over again, without bitterness, doing manual labour. Little by little he built up a new business, paid off all his creditors and left a fortune when he died. Rupert Potter was right to be proud of him.

Holidays apart, Rupert spent much of his time at his clubs and viewing exhibitions of paintings at the various London galleries. His other hobby, at which he excelled, was photography. Mrs Potter concerned herself with directing her servants in matters relating to the household and driving out in her carriage to take tea with other Kensington ladies of her class. In matters of religion both shared the Unitarianism of their parents.

Beatrix was born into that Victorian generation of the well-to-do who took little active part in the bringing up of their children. The Potters were no exception to this generally accepted rule and were content to place that responsibility in the capable Scots hands of Nurse McKenzie. The nursery, as it was known ever after to Beatrix and Bertram, her younger brother by almost six years, was situated at the top of the house and shared by both children until Bertram was old enough to go to boarding school. Beatrix, on the other hand, like all daughters of the wealthy at that time, was educated at home by a series of governesses. The nursery was not only her school room but the place where she lived and grew up, seeing her parents from time to time as appropriate and effectively leading an almost separate life from them during her childhood years. The expectation of any kind of future career as we understand the word today simply did not exist. Young ladies of her background were expected in due course to marry well, but if they remained unmarried it was their duty to stay at home and devote their lives to looking after their ageing parents. It is therefore tempting to suppose that for Beatrix her solitary childhood was a lonely one, especially after Bertram departed for boarding school and they saw each other only during the school holidays. She certainly lived a very isolated life and this undoubtedly contributed to her being abnormally shy. Her parents were rather aloof and distant, particularly

Mrs Potter, and it is fair to say that throughout her life Beatrix's relationship with her mother was never close, though she was always a dutiful daughter. Her feelings towards her father seem rather more affectionate, if formal. Only three letters written by Beatrix during her childhood years have survived and it is perhaps noteworthy that they are all written to her father.

To judge the Potters as parents by today's standards, though, is perhaps to judge them too harshly. This was the era when children were seen and not heard. Rightly or wrongly many parents displayed a stiff formality towards their children, with few if any outward signs of affection and little consideration given to their emotional needs. In turn children brought up in this way knew nothing else and consequently had little if any expectation of expressed parental love. Feelings, it seems, were not openly talked about in Victorian society. In such an emotionally airless environment it was important, therefore, to develop strategies to survive. Beatrix became expert in this.

She had learned to read, write and draw at an early age and her intelligence and quickness in learning was immediately apparent to every governess engaged in her education. One such governess was Miss Hammond, who perceived in her shy pupil a deep and sensitive interest in nature and an emerging talent in drawing and painting that she gently encouraged. This inspired in Beatrix a self-confidence which developed into an affectionate bond between them. Nevertheless, when Beatrix reached her early teens, Miss Hammond reluctantly left, declaring that her young student had outpaced the teacher.

The last governess, only three years older than Beatrix, was Miss Annie Carter who took up her post in 1883 until her marriage two years later when she left to become Mrs Annie Moore. For Beatrix, the departure of Miss Carter from her accustomed place in the nursery was keenly felt. They remained good friends however, and years later it was to Annie's son Noel that Beatrix wrote the famous Peter Rabbit picture-letter from Perthshire. Although she greatly missed Miss Carter and the friendship which had blossomed between them, Beatrix was steadily developing an inner resilience that would mature and stand her in good stead all her life. Alone now in the nursery and schoolroom she was undismayed, and life there does not seem to have been characterised by loneliness.

As a young child she had learned to read using her parents' set of the Waverley novels, hardly the easiest of texts with which to begin her reading career. 'I had had a horrid large print primer and a stodgy fat book – I think it was called *A History of the Robin Family*, by Mrs. Trimmer,' Beatrix recalled years later, writing in 1929 of her childhood reading tastes. 'I know I hated it – then I was let loose on *Rob Roy*, and spelled through a few pages painfully; then I tried *Ivanhoe* – and *The Talisman* – then I tried *Rob Roy* again; all at once I began to READ (missing the long words, of course)...'[3] For Beatrix the novels of Sir Walter Scott, which she 'read over and over',[4] were simply wonderful, filling her world with romance and adventure and setting her imagination free to roam at will. Ardent reader though she was, there was also an early and deep desire to be creative, a restless urge to use her brain and hone her faculties to the utmost. To satisfy it Beatrix later set herself challenging tests of memory such as learning Shakespearean plays by heart: 'I learnt six more or less in a year. Never felt the least strained or should not have done it.'[5] Yet even this was not enough to fulfill her creative yearning. She wanted to write too. Through her extensive reading Beatrix had discovered that Samuel Pepys had written his famous diary in shorthand using a kind of cipher code. This may well have provided the inspiration for Beatrix to also begin a secret *Journal*, and little by little she invented code writing of her own for this purpose. It is not known when she first undertook this task but she perfected it to such a degree that she was able to write it fluently at speed, and using it recorded a significant private *Journal* of some 200,000 words between 1881–97. And it seems that it *was* a private *Journal*, for she appears never to have spoken of its existence to anyone. The forgotten *Journal* lay undiscovered until 1952 and the code writing remained a mystery until solved in 1958 by Leslie Linder, the notable Potter specialist.

Whether reading or listening to tales of the supernatural brought to eerie life by Nurse McKenzie, or to stories of the life and times of her ancestors recounted in the reminiscences of her adored grandmother Mrs Edmund Potter, Beatrix had silently absorbed every last detail, retaining all in a private imagination that knew no bounds.

If there were other children in the neighbourhood of the same age as Beatrix it appears her parents did not encourage them to visit. She was not a robust child and quite small for her age so it is possible her parents considered that other children could bring germs into the house. On the other hand perhaps it never occurred to them that their daughter might welcome and enjoy company of her own age, and friends to stay for tea, especially with Bertram away at school. It seems that no playmates did ever join Beatrix for tea, not human ones at any rate. However her parents apparently had no objection to pets (at least, the conventional ones they knew of) sharing the nursery and this was just as well, for Beatrix was devoted to the animals who shared her life in the nursery at No 2 Bolton Gardens.

1.1 **A painting of 'Benjamin Bunny'
by Beatrix Potter.**

Reproduced by kind permission of
Frederick Warne & Co.

Her pets, many and varied, were her friends, ranging from mice, snails and even a pet rat, to the hedgehog and rabbits she later immortalised. They peopled her world and fed her imagination, providing the quiet companionship she liked and indeed preferred. They also acted as models for her drawing and painting, a passion that absorbed her and kept her constantly busy. This and a desire to learn as much as she could about natural history were activities she pursued with a dedication and single-minded concentration uninterrupted by other humans.

Beatrix had always loved to draw and paint, showing special aptitude from an early age. Both her parents and brother had artistic talent and Bertram, with the approval of his parents, later became an artist specialising for the most part in landscapes and avoiding anything *avant garde* of which they would not have approved. As well as being skilled in embroidery, Mrs Potter was, in her younger days before her marriage, accomplished in watercolour, painting in the fashion of the day like other young ladies of her class. As for Rupert Potter, his artistic skill (aside from his considerable photographic talent) lay chiefly in draughtsmanship, for he had little understanding of the many difficulties of painting despite his great interest in it. At any rate a good grounding in art was clearly considered essential by the Potters and, recognising their daughter's emerging artistic talent, they decided that formal drawing instruction was desirable for her. They employed a Miss Cameron for this purpose when Beatrix was 12 and drawing lessons continued until she was 17. 'I have great reason to be grateful to her, though we were not on particularly good terms for the last good while. I have learnt from her freehand, model, geometry, perspective and a little water-colour flower painting.'[6] Beatrix also had some instruction in figure drawing and oils given by a Mrs A.: 'I don't much like it, which is rather disappointing.'[7] Curiously, despite her father's wealth, the cost of these painting lessons from Mrs A. seems to have been an issue, for Beatrix recorded in her *Journal* 'Can have no more because Mrs A.'s charge is high',[8] adding 'it is tiresome, when you do get some lessons, to be taught in a way you dislike and to have to swallow your feelings out of considerations at home and there... I do wish these drawing lessons were over...'[9] As always, although she desired to learn, she also wished to express herself by painting in her own way, noting again in the privacy of her *Journal*, 'I shall paint just as I like when not with her... I am convinced it lies chiefly with oneself.'[10]

The true expression of this had been given full scope for the first time when in 1871 Rupert Potter rented, for the family holiday, Dalguise House near Dunkeld in Perthshire. At Dalguise Beatrix discovered the countryside and found there a deep and abiding love of nature. Dalguise was the starting place for all that followed.

CHAPTER TWO

'...above all,...we were again crossing
to Scotland (at twenty-five to six)...' [1]

HOLIDAYS WERE NOTHING NEW to Rupert Potter, who was used to going off on family breaks as a boy long before his own marriage. Years later therefore, with a wife and family of his own, it was natural that he should wish to continue the family holiday tradition, leaving smoky London at regular intervals for rest and relaxation in the country or at the seaside. The spring break, usually taken in March or April, was a short affair of about two weeks' duration, when the family left London for one of the popular seaside resorts such as Sidmouth, Falmouth, Eastbourne or Ilfracombe, where they stayed at lodgings. Like holiday-makers of today the Potters carefully considered where best to go. As a family they do not seem to have gone abroad, but the early spring weather was an important consideration in their choice of destination, as Beatrix recalled when she was almost 16. 'We came to Ilfracombe 3rd April 1882. There had been much discussion as to where we should go, as Papa had decided not to go to Dawlish. We had been told of lodgings at Cromer, but Mamma thought it would be very cold there and the country was dull, so she persuaded him to come here.'[2]

Journey times were considerable before The Great Western Railway abolished the Broad Gauge on 21 May 1892. After travelling from London to Falmouth on the Broad Gauge with the family on the last day of March 1892 for their Easter holiday, Beatrix wrote, 'It is a tremendous long journey, perhaps seeming longer than it is because one is less conversant with the route than with either of the lines to the North. We started at 10.15 stopping only twice (Swindon and Taunton) before reaching Exeter, and got in at six.'[3] Meanwhile, back at No 2 Bolton Gardens, London, the servants got on with spring-cleaning the house from top to bottom before the Potters resumed residence at the end of their fortnight away.

The Potters' long summer holiday was quite another matter. For many years this was spent in Scotland, beginning in late July and lasting for about three months until the end of October. Preparations were detailed and painstaking as the servants laboured to seamlessly reproduce in Scotland their employers' accustomed lifestyle at Bolton Gardens. In order to achieve this the servants came to Perthshire too. Cook was essential, and of almost equal importance was a nurse to look after the children in the early years and in later years a governess. Other key members of staff were the housekeeper and Mr Cox, their indispensable butler. So that Mr and Mrs Potter, their family and friends, could conveniently travel about as they pleased after their arrival in Perthshire, the family's own carriage and horses, coachman and groom, also travelled north on the train.

By choosing to holiday in Perthshire, Rupert Potter was again following a tradition established by his own father who, in his time, had also taken the main holiday of the year in Scotland. Every summer from 1859 until 1862 Edmund Potter had rented the spacious Kinnaird House, a dower house of the Duke of Atholl which was situated only a few miles north of Dalguise.

Set amidst beautiful grounds with wonderful views to the hills the name Kinnaird or 'Hill Head', from the Scottish Gaelic, *ceann* 'head' and *aird* 'height', reflects well its fine elevated position. Here Edmund Potter entertained his influential friends, many of them politicians, tempting his guests to join him in the north with the promise of good fishing, shooting and conversation during

2.1 Entrance to Kinnaird House, Perthshire.

the summer months. It had been a most successful blueprint and one which Rupert Potter intended to replicate almost exactly. It is possible that Rupert even travelled to Scotland himself to inspect Dalguise House before taking up the lease, for it seems that he may have been there when he received an eager undated letter from his little daughter, at home in London and excited at the prospect of a family holiday in Perthshire. In it Beatrix implores her father to send her a picture of anything nice that he encounters at Dalguise and also to write with news of the dogs and of Dalguise itself. The charming little letter ends affectionately with Beatrix sending her father a kiss before signing her name, very formally, H. B. Potter.

Rupert Potter was certainly in wintry Perthshire in 1874 for on 2 March he wrote to his wife from Dalguise, and also to seven-year-old Beatrix. 'The white cat from the Stable lives in the house and has kept away the rats and mice very well all winter. There are some snow-drops on the lawn but the trees are all bare and no bunnies are to be seen...'4 It is intriguing to speculate whether details contained in this lovingly written letter from her father and received by Beatrix at a time when Dalguise was becoming the centre of her world subconsciously lodged in her memory, emerging years later as the white cat who sat by the goldfish pond in *The Tale of Peter Rabbit*. Throughout folklore snowy white cats have symbolised the Spirit. Nurse McKenzie excelled at telling wonderful stories rich in folklore and the supernatural, drawn from the mists of her own Scots upbringing, which enthralled Beatrix as a child. Furthermore a white cat is quite a rare sight, especially so when employed as a creature of the farmyard charged with keeping troublesome rats and mice under control and living in the drawing room instead of the stable. Perhaps, therefore, it is not so surprising after all that whilst most children would draw a brown, tabby, ginger or even black cat sitting beside a goldfish pond Beatrix, perhaps remembering that long-ago letter from her father at Dalguise and Nurse McKenzie's stories, would choose to draw a white cat.

One wonders, however, what circumstances prevailed to bring Rupert so far from home in the depths of the Scottish winter other than to satisfy himself that all was in order at Dalguise before renewing the lease which would again commence in May. Rupert Potter was nothing if not thorough and, wealthy though he was, he would not for an instant have contemplated wasting money leasing Dalguise House had it not fulfilled his requirements. Clearly though, Rupert did like what he found for he and his family travelled north from London to enjoy the summer pleasures and guaranteed home comforts of Dalguise House.

2.2 **Beatrix Potter – a childhood photograph taken by her father.**

Reproduced by kind permission of The Beatrix Potter Society. Photograph by Rupert Potter

There is no *Journal* to enable us to follow Beatrix through those magical, cherished Dalguise years for she did not begin to keep it until November 1881. In that same year Dalguise House, for the first time in 11 years, was no longer available for lease and so it is from photographs, letters and the many scattered *Journal* references after that date that we are able to piece together and distil a little of the essence that stole her heart.

The Potters' annual unrecorded expedition to Perthshire would have varied little year by year from 1871. By 1884 however Beatrix, in the privacy of her *Journal*, was noting every detail of that much-loved railway journey to Perthshire, which over the years she had come to know so well:

> Peterborough we saw very well, but I was not so much struck by it as by Durham and York, not because the latter were finer... as on account of the faded light...[5] Holy Island was a little disappointing, it was so flat, but the sands were pretty with a red cart coming towards the Island. The coast was very fine after this, but still more so after crossing the border.[6]

From the beginning she recorded the scene from her railway carriage with the eye of an artist and the joy of the homecoming exile:

> I was much struck by Newcastle, the high bridge, the smoke and the *coaly Tyne*... But Berwick was one of the most interesting places we passed. The old town with its walls perched above the harbour, and broad river where the salmon-netting was going on... but, above all, the fact that we were again crossing to Scotland (at twenty-five to six)...[7]

And on another journey, in 1892:

> We stopped through some delay near Dunbar, opposite a sleeping Station Garden full of rose bushes weighed down with wet.[8]
>
> The Bass and North Berwick Bay presented a curious and beautiful effect through layers of cloud against a silver sea and sky...[9] I kept awake for the cold, flat expanse of Loch Leven with its strange heavy hills, and then slept till Perth.[10]

Beatrix recalled clearly the hustle and bustle as the London train pulled into Perth station and how she 'washed in uncommonly cold water'[11] there. She remembered too

> the old first-class waiting room with a rather greedy relish as a child. It was one of the rare occasions when one was allowed to eat ham and eggs. From the arrangement of the local trains in those days, we had several hours in Perth, a leisurely interval in the middle of the remove.[12]

2.3 **Loch Leven**

For the Potters, arrival in Perth with its gracious spires, its wide green Inches⋆ and the magnificent River Tay close by, signified journey's end almost in sight and the start of their holiday in the beautiful Perthshire countryside.

⋆The North and South Inch are two extensive areas of renowned parkland in the centre of Perth beside the River Tay. The word Inch is derived from the Scottish Gaelic word Innis meaning 'island' or 'water-meadow'.

2.4 **South Inch, Perth**

CHAPTER THREE

'It is strange what a wrong impression of the length of time one gets from history, so many things happen in a century.' [1]

THE SMALL TOWN OF Dunkeld, gateway to the Central Highlands, is situated on the southern edge of the Grampian mountains. It is a peaceful place set amidst a beautiful backdrop of steeply wooded slopes, craggy in places, which subtly change colour with the weather and the passing seasons. From the walls of its ancient cathedral broad lawns and fine trees border the majestic River Tay, Scotland's longest river. A historic little town, it is hardly surprising that visitors are attracted to its tranquil setting. The Potters certainly were.

From earliest times people have come to Dunkeld. The name *Dun Chaillean* (Dunkeld) may be interpreted as Fortress of the Caledonians, or as Fortress of the Culdees. The Caledonians were a tribe of Picts who established a stronghold at Dunkeld during the first millennium. The Culdees or followers of Columba were monks who came later, around 700AD. In 848AD, faced with the terror of Viking raids on their monastery on the tiny Hebridean island of Iona, the monks brought the precious bones of St Columba from there to the relative safety of Dunkeld. When brigands and wolves roamed the surrounding countryside this little settlement must have been a welcome sanctuary for weary travellers. There had been a bishopric in Dunkeld since the 12th century and in the early part of that century building of the Cathedral began. Gradually the church became rich and powerful, until the Reformation changed all that and consequently, in 1560, the cathedral was deliberately damaged and almost destroyed. Over three centuries later when the Potters came to worship in Dunkeld Cathedral, Beatrix described in her *Journal* some of the changes to the once-glorious interior of the building.

> The portion of the Cathedral where public worship is held is walled out of the old building in an arbitrary ugly fashion. It is very plain inside, and down below intensely cold. We generally sit in the west gallery, the high old pews distressingly covered with hieroglyphics. They are open under the seat, and *non non quam* descends a peppermint, hop, hop, hop, from tier to tier.[2]

In Beatrix's hands, one can almost feel the silent anguish of that member of the congregation during the deafening descent of the confection through the echoing silence. Notwithstanding, Beatrix continued to quietly survey the scene from her cold pew, noting the high pulpit and facing it the pew of the Duchess of Atholl,

3.1 **The River Tay from Telford's bridge at Dunkeld. The Cathedral can be seen among the trees on the right.**

covered in a way that always reminds me inappositely of a grand-stand. The Duchess is away from home, but the servants are ranged in order. Over the front stands the Atholl coat of arms, its two wild men and savage feudal motto – "Forth, Fortune, and fill the Fetters" – about as appropriate in a modern Kirk as the gigantic broken figure of the black wolf of Badenoch in the vestibule.[3]

The Wolf of Badenoch was Alexander Stewart, Earl of Buchan, the notorious son of King Robert II who, in 1390, burned down Elgin Cathedral and was consequently excommunicated from the Church. He eventually repented and at his death in 1405 was buried beneath the altar at Dunkeld Cathedral.

Beatrix also noted the continuation of the old custom of locking the doors during the service. 'I wonder what happens if anyone faints, not that I imagine a native capable of such an indiscretion.'[4] Such thoughts lead her to observe one or two of the congregation during the long sermon. The Minister Mr Rutherford in his high pulpit 'earnest, pale and foxy-haired, with a pointed beard and decent Geneva bands'.[5] Then,

> Perched just below him... is the Precentor, a fine big man with a bullet-head, chubby red face, retroussé nose and a voice like a bull. He is the Birnam schoolmaster. He pitches all the tunes too high, and it seems the etiquette that he begins a note before the congregation, and prolongs the last note after them in a long buzz.[6]

Finally Beatrix observes 'the bottle-nosed Dr. Dickson... in staring plaid trousers, and a perfectly new pair of tan driving gloves'.[7] Later, Beatrix discovered the reason for Dr Dickson's affliction; it seemed to be common knowledge locally that 'His nose, though frightful, is a source of income, for it was injured in a chemical explosion in Paris, and he "gets so much a week from it".'[8]

By the 17th century religious and political turmoil in Scotland was rife. Following the Battle of Killiecrankie in 1689, fought in the narrow, heavily wooded Pass of Killiecrankie just north of Dunkeld, the town itself was besieged by opposing Jacobite and Government forces and burnt to the ground. Only three houses and the remnants of the Cathedral survived and it was not until well into the 18th century that rebuilding slowly began with the inclusion of the 'ugly' additions Beatrix noted. In a *Journal* entry made in January 1882 Beatrix reflected,

> It is strange what a wrong impression of the length of time one gets from history, so many things happen in a century.[9a] Old Mr. Horn used to say he talked to a Blacksmith whose father was in the battle of Killiecrankie.[9b]

Royalist Jacobite forces led by John Graham of Claverhouse, Viscount Dundee, better known in history and ballad as Bonnie Dundee, defeated the troops of William of Orange at Killiecrankie. However, Dundee was badly injured during the fighting and died later at nearby Blair Castle. The name Killiecrankie means 'Wood of aspen trees' from the Scottish Gaelic *coille* 'wood' and *creitheannich* 'aspens'.

As weekly markets and fairs became established in Dunkeld it became increasingly evident that a bridge replacing the ferry across the Tay was needed at the town itself, although previous attempts to achieve this had been swept away by the power of the river. In 1728 General Wade, as part of his road-building programme for the Highlands, proposed to build a bridge at Dunkeld but his

3.2 **Thomas Telford's bridge at Dunkeld.**

plans were given a lukewarm reception by the Duke of Atholl who owned both the ferry and the surrounding lands. Wade duly revised his plans and built his splendid bridge across the Tay at Aberfeldy two years later. In September 1892 Beatrix took a drive beside the River Braan 'with the pony and camera, intending to take General Wade's Bridge above Kennacoil'.[10] Unfortunately 'the vapours were too heavy'[11] that day for successful photography. It was the great civil engineer Thomas Telford (1757–1834) who finally designed and built the fine seven-span bridge across the Tay at Dunkeld which is still used today.

Most of the money to build it was provided by the Duke of Atholl but when it opened in 1809 tolls continued to be levied, triggering riots. These continued periodically over the next 60 years until the County Council assumed responsibility for the bridge and tolls finally ceased.

By 1842 the Square and Market Cross, the latter complete with jougs, iron collars for the punishment of wrongdoers, had been rebuilt and the town felt sufficiently confident to welcome Queen Victoria and Prince Albert during their Royal Progress through Perthshire. The Queen was delighted with her visit and this Royal seal of approval did much to put Dunkeld and the surrounding countryside on the map.

Much associated with the Victorian era was the coming of the railways and in 1856 Birnam station opened, bringing to an end the relative obscurity of the area. Hardy travellers, though few in number, had been making their way to the

Highlands for the express purpose of exploration long before the dawn of the railways. Dr Johnson and his biographer James Boswell were travelling in Scotland together in 1773, subsequently publishing their impressions. Thomas Pennant had already published (in 1770) his book *A Tour of Scotland*, which was influential in bringing the natural beauties and grandeur of Scotland to the attention of the public. The Potters may well have owned a copy of this book and packed it for holiday reading in Perthshire. The railway age enabled tourists with sufficient leisure and means to follow, with comparative ease, Queen Victoria's fashionable example and see for themselves the glories of the North.

When the Potters disembarked from the train at Birnam station in 1871 they no doubt had much to occupy their immediate attention, Mrs Potter's mind concentrating perhaps on household matters which had occurred to her during the journey. These she would bring to the immediate attention of her servants directly they arrived at Dalguise, not to mention any shortcomings she perceived in the arrangements thus far. Mr Potter, possibly a little agitated on the station platform, was concerned to see that his fragile, expensive and precious photographic equipment was being handled carefully, as he expected it to be, by station staff.

For Beatrix, excited but waiting patiently, it was simply glorious to be in Perthshire and at last a mere stone's throw from Dalguise. 'Before the railway was made,' she recalled,

3.3 **Birnam railway station**

people said it would frighten all game out of the valley, but it has not the slightest effect upon it, except that extinct animal the brown hare, which had a trick of using the line as a highway like the other natives, and when it met a train sometimes lost its life through indecision, as cats do in London.[12]

In fact game did not seem to be in the least alarmed by the movement of loco-motives, as Beatrix observed for herself.

I remember a partridge's nest with an incredible number of eggs, in the hollow between the two sleepers in the goods siding at Dalguise, where trucks were constantly shunted over the bird's head. It is common to see roe deer from the train, they lift their heads and then go on feeding. There are many in the wood at the back judging by the tracks...[13]

Beatrix may well have packed for the holidays Lewis Caroll's *Alice's Adventures in Wonderland* to read again in her very own Perthshire wonderland. The book had been given to her when she was six or seven years old and she had found it captivating, adding its treasures to those already carefully stored away and kept bright in her imagination. There were also other perfect stories for her to enjoy again and dream about in Scotland, such as the romance and history of Sir Walter Scott's *Rob Roy* and *The Fair Maid of Perth*. No less real and enthralling for Beatrix were the stories of long ago from Nurse McKenzie's own country, recounted by Nurse herself in her lilting Scots accent beside the nursery fire on dark winter nights. These too were of heroic romantic feats, battles lost and won, legends and the supernatural, for Nurse had 'a firm belief in witches, fairies and the creed of the terrible John Calvin (the creed rubbed off, but the fairies remained)...'[14] To Beatrix, all these adventures became even more vivid north of the border.

Everything was romantic in my imagination. The woods were peopled by the myste-rious good folk. The Lords and Ladies of the last century walked with me along the overgrown paths, and picked the old-fashioned flowers among the box and rose hedges of the garden. Half believing the picturesque superstitions of the district, seeing my own fancies so clearly that they became true to me, I lived in a separate world.[15]

All of this and of course her indispensable paint box and pencils came with Beatrix to Perthshire.

Beatrix was five when she first saw Dalguise House, an elegant residence with many windows and chimneys.

Situated amid well-tended lawns and gardens, the grounds extend back into dark woods covering low hills behind the house. Its long driveway meets a narrow but quiet public road where pheasants have time to cross at leisure. Scottish blackface sheep and Highland cattle graze pastures beyond the hawthorn hedges, wild roses and birch trees of the sparsely scattered township of Dalguise. The word Dalguise or 'Haugh of fir' is derived from the Scottish Gaelic *Dail* meaning 'haugh' or 'meadow' and *giuthas* meaning 'fir', a perfect description of the place. In warm weather cattle stand knee deep in the sparkling waters of the River Tay bordering the grazings and in season salmon fishermen cast their lines in the cold fast-flowing waters. Northwards the high hills change colour as the year moves on. Beatrix observed this scene around Dalguise House and its environs every year until she was 17.

The bees hum round the flowers, the air is laden with the smell of roses, Sandy lies in his accustomed place against the doorstep. Now and then a party of swallows cross the lawn and over the house, screaming shrilly, and the deep low of the cattle comes answering one another across the valley, borne on the summer breeze which sweeps down through the woods from the heathery moors.[16]

She would still recognise it today.

Drawing and painting had absorbed Beatrix from her earliest years and every aspect of natural history fascinated her. From old-fashioned natural history volumes in her father's library she copied illustrations with an intensity, dedication and growing talent which for a child was noteworthy. With her nurse or governess she visited the South Kensington Museum, as it was called in its early days before it became the Victoria and Albert Museum, as well as the new British Museum of Natural History. If her guardians sometimes became a little weary of these visits, Beatrix never did. The museums housed in their glass cases vast collections of every animal and plant that could be imagined and provided endless subjects for her to draw. But the exhibits were just that, interesting but inanimate objects. Beautiful, fascinating and lifelike though they were behind their polished glass enclosures, they were lifeless no matter how fascinating. How often did Beatrix wonder what it would be like to see a real live golden eagle soaring above rocky crags or a magnificent wild red deer stag running like the wind? Dalguise and the surrounding countryside answered her dreams. The richness of the wildlife there dazzled her. It was a revelation.

CHAPTER FOUR

'Scudding showers and the wind that shakes the barley.' [1]

COMFORTABLY SETTLED AT Dalguise House, Mr and Mrs Potter concentrated their attention on their holiday. For Beatrix, used to London and the strict unvarying routines of daily life at Bolton Gardens, Dalguise and the surrounding area offered a landscape she instinctively preferred. It also brought a feeling, which persisted and strengthened as she grew older, that here was a better, more meaningful way of life.

In London, Beatrix was quite often ill with colds and other childhood ailments. In Perthshire she flourished in the healthy outdoor life and she revelled in the freedom of the peaceful countryside and the beauty it revealed to her in so many different ways. It was the perfect place for her to get close to nature and study it to her heart's delight. She absorbed every detail of things she saw or found in hedgerow, woodland, riverbank and garden.

A page from her earliest surviving sketch-book inscribed '1875 Dalguise' shows a selection of caterpillars, one crawling up a stem, others on leaves, which she painted when she was nine years old.

This little sketch-book was home-made from a type of paper often used to line shelves. Beatrix sewed sheets of it together to make a little book measuring six and a half inches by six inches and then wrote on the cover in pencil the title 'Dalguise, Dunkeld, Perthshire'. Within the covers, the choice of subjects and the careful drawing of them clearly illustrates her desire to portray, as accurately as she could, the small wild creatures and plants she had found. Furthermore on the back of the page featuring the caterpillars she recorded, with the eye of a naturalist, observations of her subjects. These included details such as the feeding habits and habitat of each caterpillar, together with a description of each one and the time of year they were likely to be found. For one, she notes 'The caterpillar eats sloe, it is a rare moth'[2] and for another, her theory about what the caterpillar might eat: 'I dont [sic] know what it eats, but I think it is the flowering nettle.'[3]

This first sketch-book also contains her drawings of birds' eggs and butter-flies, the countryside around Dalguise and the garden of the house itself. She loved flowers and always gathered a few from the wayside to bring back to the house to draw when the family were out for country walks. The bright foxglove of high summer, abundant around Dalguise, was a favourite wild flower

4.1 **Caterpillars painted by Beatrix Potter at Dalguise in 1875.**

Reproduced by kind permission of Frederick Warne & Co.

included in her sketch-book when she was young. The memory of those tall mauve spires remained and years later she painted them again in *The Tale of Jemima Puddle-Duck*.

From the time of their marriage Rupert and Helen Potter maintained a busy social life. Mr Potter, a member of the Reform Club, was regularly to be found there although he was also a member of the Athenaeum. Mrs Potter had her circle of lady friends to call upon and the Potters also liked to give elaborate dinner parties. Coming on holiday to Dalguise however did not mean they suddenly cut themselves off from their circle of friends, with whom Rupert Potter relished discussion of painting and art, politics and poetry. Friends such as John Bright the Liberal politician, who had also been a friend of Rupert's father, and the artist John Everett Millais, both keen fishermen, frequently accepted the Potters' invitations to pack their fishing rods and join the family at Dalguise. Millais often brought his wife and daughters with him, as Mrs Potter welcomed the ladies' company, and the journey to Dalguise from the Millais' family home near Perth was a short one. Lord and Lady Manners, later seventh Duke and Duchess of Rutland, who lived at St Mary's Tower in Birnam, were also invited and warmly welcomed to the Potters' holiday idyll, as was Lord Houghton.

At Dalguise, as in London, there were not many children for Beatrix to play with. As usual though, absorbed in her own interests, magnified now that she was at Dalguise, she had the perfect companion in Sandy, a brown Scotch terrier, who was her first dog and whose company she liked. Together they explored the countryside. Sandy, absorbed with his own interests in the undergrowth, was content like his young mistress to pause long and often on their leisurely rambles before slowly returning to the house with her in time for tea. It would be several years before Beatrix's brother Bertram would be old enough to join them. There was, however, one particular friend of her parents, known to her father through his Manchester Unitarian associations, of whom Beatrix was especially fond. He was the Unitarian minister William Gaskell, and fortunately he was a frequent and most welcome visitor at Dalguise. Beatrix and Bertram loved his company, and he theirs, sharing their interests in animals and the countryside. A man of great compassion, Gaskell along with his wife Elizabeth worked tirelessly for social reform in Manchester, where his parishioners were mostly impoverished textile workers. A brilliant lecturer and academic, William Gaskell was responsible for establishing, amongst other things, evening classes at Owens College. He also taught at the Working Man's College in Manchester. Shocked by the terrible poverty she witnessed, Elizabeth wrote a novel, *Mary Barton: A Tale of Manchester Life*, which brought to public attention the plight of working people living in industrial towns and cities. This book and others she wrote subsequently brought the name of Mrs Gaskell to prominence, making her one of Britain's most popular novelists. Although a widower in his early 70s by the time he visited the Potters at Dalguise, Gaskell's influence on, and work for, the people of Manchester was not forgotten. Beatrix never forgot his gentle influence either, recalling years later,

> Oh how plainly I see it again. He is sitting comfortably in the warm sunshine on the doorstep at Dalguise, in his grey coat and old felt hat. The newspaper lies on his knees, suddenly he looks up with his gentle smile. There are sounds of pounding

4.2 **Mr William Gaskell and Beatrix Potter at Dalguise.**

Reproduced by kind permission of The Beatrix Potter Society. Photograph by Rupert Potter.

footsteps. The blue-bottles whiz off the path. A little girl in a print frock and striped stockings bounds to his side and offers him a bunch of meadowsweet. He just says "thank you, dear", and puts his arm round her.[4]

The sheer abundance of wild flowers at Dalguise delighted the nine-year-old Beatrix. They filled the countryside, spilling over from every wayside hedge and ditch, painting the landscape in a wealth of seasonal colour. Wild roses, periwinkles and narcissus were all carefully studied and lovingly copied into her sketch-book and now she also made a point of signing and dating her work too.

Holidays or no, standards of dress were not relaxed very much and Beatrix was far from delighted at this irksome aspect of her new-found freedom. 'What I wore was absurdly uncomfortable; white *piqué* starched frocks just like Tenniel's *Alice in Wonderland*, and cotton stockings striped round and round like a zebra's legs.'[5a] Even her hairstyle, which Nurse brushed straight back to be held in place by a plain band, was uncomfortable as far as Beatrix was concerned, 'black velvet on Sundays, and either black or brown ribbon week days... I remember the bands fastened with a bit of elastic, looped over a button behind the ear; it hurt.'[5b]

If she was permitted little choice over what clothing was regarded by Nurse as suitable for her, Beatrix determined to improve the lot of her dearest friend Mr Gaskell in this respect by knitting him a comforter for Christmas. He was clearly touched and delighted with the gift and in his letter of thanks to Beatrix said, 'Big as I am I know I could not have done it one-tenth as well. Every time I put it round my neck – which during this weather will be every day – I shall be sure to think of you.'[6]

On another occasion, whilst continuing his holiday in Scotland following a visit to Dalguise, Mr Gaskell wrote to Beatrix on a subject he knew to be close to her heart – her beloved pets. 'A rabbit lying among the heather reminded me of Tommy, who I hope is taking his food properly, and doing well. If you think he remembers me, please give him my kind regards.'[7] For Beatrix, the fond remembrance of the little rabbit in the heather far away in the Scottish hills that Mr Gaskell had described for her, the memory of dear Mr Gaskell himself wearing the comforter she had carefully knitted for him when she was eight and which he proudly wore against the cold, the many happy days they had spent together at Dalguise, all remained joyfully in her mind.

As usual Beatrix was busy with her paintbrush and pencil, but for the first time a page in her sketch-book dated 21 March 1876 shows a blending together of nature and fantasy. Rabbits, walking upright, are wearing colourful mufflers and warm hats, mittens, jackets and boots. Some are having fun in the snow, pushing each other on sledges, while others are testing their skill on ice skates. In another painting of the same date similarly clad rabbits are holding on to their hats in the wind and one wearing spectacles is holding on tightly to his umbrella which has been blown inside out. On the opposite page to this little sketch is a painting of an arched bridge over a river with high hills rising in the distance. Although only two spans are shown it is not too fanciful to see the likeness between Beatrix's bridge and that built by Thomas Telford over the River Tay at Dunkeld and used by the Potters themselves when visiting the town. Although there is no evidence to say this is the case it is reasonable and pleasant to speculate that happy holidays in the Dalguise area inspired this little group of early paintings.

Rupert Potter's skill as a photographer is apparent in the many photographs he took during Beatrix's early years. Still in its infancy, photography was a lengthy process requiring subjects to remain motionless for considerable periods to ensure a clear image. Mrs Potter and Beatrix were patient sitters in this respect and later Bertram was also included in family groups. These occasionally show Rupert himself in delayed action shots. Mrs Potter's resemblance to Queen Victoria is quite striking and well seen in Rupert's studies of his wife. Friends who joined the Potters on holiday were all, sooner or later, subjects for Rupert's hobby and solemnly posed for the camera. Portraiture seems to have been Rupert's favourite aspect of the photographers' art. His talent was admired and appreciated by his friend, John Everett Millais who often asked him for photographs to use as a reference for background details whilst working at his easel in his studio. At Millais' request Rupert also photographed for him many distinguished sitters. 'Mr. Millais says the professionals aren't fit to hold a candle to papa,'[8] Beatrix recorded with pride in her Journal. Her father was evidently delighted and even a little flattered by the compliment paid to him by Millais for as Beatrix noted, 'Papa says, it is a pleasure to see someone who is obliged to you for your trouble.'[9] The long family holidays in Perthshire afforded Rupert wonderful scope for the development of his photographic interest which, when she was older, he shared with Beatrix.

For the moment Rupert was pleased to encourage his little daughter's artistic talent and take an interest in her delight in nature study. In time, Bertram was included too.

The Potters' annual holidays in Perthshire happily included two family anniversaries. The first, in July, was Beatrix's birthday.

I remember so clearly – as clearly as the brightness of rich Scotch sunshine on the threadbare carpet – the morning I was ten years old – and my father gave me Mrs. Blackburn's book of birds, drawn from nature, for my birthday present. I remember the dancing expectation and knocking at their bedroom door, it was a Sunday morning, before breakfast. I kept it in the drawing room cupboard, only to be taken out after I had washed my grimy little hands under that wonderful curved brass tap, which, being lifted, let loose the full force of ice-cold amber-water from the hills. The book was bound in scarlet with a gilt edge. I danced about the house with pride, never palled.[10]

The second celebratory date that occurred during their stays at Dalguise was Rupert and Helen's wedding anniversary on 8 August. It is not known whether they specially marked the occasion but, as they enjoyed giving dinner parties at home in No 2 Bolton Gardens, London, there is no reason to suppose that they would not celebrate it with friends from their usual circle whom they had invited to Dalguise.

Sarah Harper, the Potters' kitchen maid and later cook, had fallen in love in Perthshire with Duncan McDonald, the estate gamekeeper at Tulliemet. The Potters had stayed at Tulliemet for the summer of 1870 (Beatrix, then four years old, could remember crawling under an old horse-hair sofa there) and subsequently Sarah had accepted Duncan's proposal of marriage. 'I remember,' Beatrix wrote years later, recalling Sarah's preparations to leave London for married life in Scotland,

being taken up into the attic as a child to finger her lilac silk dress. He was a fine looking man [Duncan McDonald] and she had £200 of savings. I am glad to say she has this yet, my father being one trustee, but I should think the income is very bare.[11]

Perhaps personal happiness in Perthshire had inspired Sarah too, albeit in a different way from Beatrix, to create a few truly Scottish delicacies for her employers' anniversaries and dinner parties before she finally left their service. Cock-a-leekie, for instance, was a soup popular in royal palaces and humbler abodes since the 16th century. As owners of the Waverley novels this dish may well have appealed to the Potters, since in the last line of Scott's *The Fortunes of Nigel* King James VI and I declares, 'Come my lords and lieges, let us all to dinner for the cock-a-leekie is a-cooling.'

Tweed Kettle probably featured on the menu in Perthshire. A very old traditional recipe for cooking salmon, during the 19th century it was popular in country houses in the valley of the River Tweed (another great salmon river in

4.3 Beatrix Potter with her brother Bertram.

Reproduced by kind permission of The Beatrix Potter Society. Photograph by Rupert Potter.

the Scottish Borders) where as the name suggests it had its origin. Sir Walter Scott may have enjoyed the dish, which when made for the Potters with salmon fresh from the River Tay would be equally delicious. Rupert Potter titled one of his photographs *After the Salmon Fishing*; it was taken on the lawn at Dalguise House and displays the day's catch of two large salmon. For dessert perhaps Sarah prepared a dish of cranachan using newly picked local raspberries and served with freshly whipped cream, or the most royal dish of all, Atholl Brose, served to Queen Victoria herself during her Perthshire Progress in 1842, from a quart cup which belonged to Niel Gow (1727–1807) the famous fiddler who lived at nearby Inver. Minus the celebrated quart cup, the Potters' friends would have been hard pressed to refuse such tempting invitations garnished with good conversation.

One guest that Beatrix remembered vividly was Sir William Brown. Perhaps this was because of a single reminiscence of his which struck a chord in her imagination concerning her childhood hero and author of the Waverley novels: '...he remembered to have seen Sir Walter [Scott] walking along Princes Street [in Edinburgh]; a man that men turned to look after; a lame man walking rather hurriedly.'[12]

Rupert and his gentlemen friends eagerly anticipated the grouse shooting, which commenced in August on the Glorious Twelfth followed by the partridge and pheasant season. Then there was deer stalking and shooting, permitted from 1 September, and with excellent fishing to be had on the River Tay they were well catered for. When the weather was clement the ladies joined them for picnics, as did Beatrix and Bertram.

With each successive summer holiday in Perthshire, Bertram was taking an ever-greater interest in the activities of his fascinating sister. Like Beatrix he was interested in nature, drawing and painting and keeping pets. It was not long therefore before he was accompanying Beatrix on her expeditions and playing a full part in all their explorations together.

CHAPTER FIVE

'I remember every stone, every tree, the scent of the heather,…
the murmuring of the wind through the fir trees.' [1]

BEATRIX WAS ALMOST SIX years old when her brother Walter Bertram was
born on 14 March 1872. By the time he was old enough to be a companion to her
she had already discovered some of the many secrets of the Dalguise countryside.
She did not yet write about the things she saw but their influence informed her
outlook as she grew up. To an observant child like Beatrix, nothing escaped her
notice in this country of enchantment. And there was so much to notice for those
who chose to look. The stone cottages and farms of the district for instance
seemed to blend into and belong to the landscape and from that landscape the
people made a hard living. Gardens were planted to feed families and yet still
managed somehow to bloom with a homely beauty. There was something
peaceful in the way the brown hens scratched for their living around the cottage
doors and a simple satisfaction in the sight of their warm eggs gathered in a
basket. The dignity and powerful beauty of heavy horses returning homewards
with the ploughman after a day's work in the field was always a sight worth
pausing for. When the blacksmith was at work in the smiddy the hiss and the
steam, the ring of hammer on anvil, the smell of iron on hoof could fill a
watching child with wonder and perhaps thoughts of romantic lines that only
Sir Walter Scott could pen.

> O, young Lochinvar is come out of the west,
> Through all the wide Border his steed was the best;
> And save his good broadsword he weapons had none,
> He rode all unarm'd and he rode all alone.
> So faithful in love, and so dauntless in war,
> There never was knight like the young Lochinvar.

The local blacksmith said that good luck was held in horseshoes and spoke of
heroic King Robert the Bruce, who had ridden to victory an ancestor of one of
those strong sure-footed Highland ponies, or garrons as they were called, long
ago at the battle of Bannockburn. Other scenes from farmyard and field would have
been familiar to Beatrix too. There was the clang of milk churns full of frothing new
milk, eyed with longing by the farmyard cats from their window-ledge perches
in the dairy. Soon there would come that miraculous flick-flack moment when
the pure white milk turned to pale creamy butter at the hands of the dairy-maid

who turned the handle of the wooden butter churn. There was the time of year when the sheep were gathered for shearing. Then the wise and faithful Border collies, responding like quicksilver to every whistled command from their shepherds, worked eagerly until at last the flocks were safely gathered in.

If the season were kind golden sheaves of ripe oats would gradually cover the little fields around Dalguise with whispering goodness. Indeed Dr Johnson once famously observed, 'Oats. A grain, which in England is generally given to horses, but in Scotland supports the people.' Perhaps the good doctor did not realise just how delicious a bowl of well-made creamy, nourishing porridge could be and it is very likely that porridge featured on the Potters' breakfast table at Dalguise, as it did on every other for miles around. Perhaps those Perthshire harvest scenes were in her mind in October 1899 when Beatrix painted *Golden Corn*, portraying mice instead of people busy in the harvest field. The picture has a partial border of oats.

She again recalled the harvest fields of Perthshire when visiting Woodfield in Hertfordshire during August 1883.

> A little of Grandpapa's oats in. Wheat getting ripe. When we came I was very disappointed with the stiff green heads, like a forest of asparagus, but now when the golden corn is beginning to bend it is much prettier, though nothing like the bonny barley and oats up north.[2]

The seemingly harmonious flow of Perthshire life measured out in so many unremarkable ways felt right and enduring to Beatrix, and although it was perhaps a feeling she did not yet fully understand in childhood, still the memory of it stayed with her.

To Beatrix the country people who lived there were different too. She liked the sound of their lilting Scots voices and turns of phrase and, young as she was, she noticed that like herself, they were a reserved race. She could not remember when, but in time she became friends with many of these kind and courteous people, such as the Geddes family and the Cleghorns, who seemed to know so much about the countryside around them and their native land. Old James Malloch, a retired master-mason who lived with his unmarried sister, was one such person. Always clad in hodden grey with a walking stick in his hand and a soft felt hat on his head, Beatrix and Bertram often encountered him on his rambles in the woods. He was always so 'glaad'[3] to see them and they would walk with him listening to his wonderful stories of 'caves and whisky-stills'.[4] James was acquainted with the Potters and could occasionally be seen sauntering along the driveway at Dalguise House in the hope that he would be asked to pose in a photograph. Folklore, knowledge about local animals and plants, and history, spoken of as though events centuries old had happened only yesterday, formed a natural backdrop to peoples' lives in Perthshire. Such knowledge however was not always to be found in books. It was said, for example, that wild goats were expert in killing adders (*Vipera berus*), Britain's only poisonous snake, as well as banishing evil spirits from mountain tops. Indeed the Gaelic word for goat, *Gobhar* (pronounced gowar), occurs throughout the Highlands in hill names such as Carn nan Gobhar (Hill of the Goats). Craigvinean forest, near Dunkeld, created in the 18th century with larch seed brought back from the Alps, has a Gaelic origin meaning the Crag of the Goats. Furthermore it was said in folklore that goats could forecast weather, although this was debatable! It *was* an established fact however that billie goat beards were used to decorate the sporrans of Highland regiments. Knowledge like this was fascinating to a curious child. It hinted at the marvellous. It required to be pondered over and

5.2 **Beatrix and Bertram Potter at Dalguise. Their father has included himself in this photograph.**

Reproduced by kind permission of The Beatrix Potter Society. Photograph by Rupert Potter.

contemplated and perhaps privately Beatrix did just that. Recalling the wonderful, romantic stories that her beloved Grandmama Potter had often related about the gallantry of the Jacobites and the handsome Bonnie Prince Charlie, Beatrix, always interested in the folklore of the district, may well have learned of the important part played in Jacobite fortunes by the humble mole. In 1702 William of Orange died following a fall from his horse which had stumbled on a mole-hill. Thereafter Jacobites everywhere raised their glasses and toasted 'the little gentleman in black velvet'. Although the activities of Mr Mole (*Talpa europaea*) were not welcomed by the gardeners at Dalguise House, one wonders if that story was in her mind when, years later in August 1892, Beatrix gently caricatured as a mole Dr John Chisholm Culbard, MD, MRCS. He was the local doctor in the district from 1857–1901 and when needed he attended the Potters when they were on holiday in Perthshire. In her *Journal* entry of 20 August 1892, Beatrix recorded an incident where her mother had caught her heel on the doorstep of Miss Anderson's shop in nearby Birnam and fallen. Mrs Potter had

> cut her elbow badly, to the bone. Went with her to Dr. Culbard, who was kind and very fat and snuffy. I did not distinguish myself, indeed retired precipitately into the garden, and had some difficulty in avoiding whisky. However, we all had tea by way of a com-promise, Dr. Culbard tucking in his table-napkin by way of a bib, and cutting a great slice of bread and apple jelly.[5]

For the present however Beatrix and now Bertram too were wholly absorbed in every aspect of the natural history of Dalguise. This interest greatly pleased their father, who encouraged them in their explorations and took an interest in their finds and the drawings they made of them.

As far as Mrs Potter was concerned, wild flowers, pinecones, butterflies and the like were most agreeable, *clean* things for 'B' and 'Bertie' (the family's pet name for Bertram) to pick and collect and therefore ideal subjects for them to draw and paint. Mrs Potter approved, especially as far as Beatrix was concerned, because flower painting was a 'must' for any accomplished Victorian girl. Mrs Potter also expected Nurse to ensure that when the children accompanied the adults on nature walks or fishing picnics by the River Tay they were always spick and span. And indeed, properly turned out as their mother expected to see them, Beatrix and Bertram gathered wayside flowers, grasses and twigs whilst out with the adults to take back to the house to paint. As they walked both children noted the birds they saw and heard and became better and better at identifying each species, knowledge they had acquired from a nursery well-stocked with books. Sometimes a dainty skylark would alight on a nearby fence post before ascending and soaring until hardly more than a tiny spot in the roof of the tall blue sky, all the while pouring forth its clear, musical song. Sometimes a jewelled cock pheasant would emerge cautiously at the margin of the wood before running swiftly to cover again with a strident 'korrk-kok' and a brief whirr of flapping wings. In the fields by the River Tay the long wispy crests of lapwing and their head-long plunges during acrobatic flight made them easy for the children to identify. Similarly the long orange-red bill and stout pink legs of oystercatchers made for instant identification and if the flock was out of sight their shrill 'kleep, kleep' call was unmistakable to Beatrix and Bertram. Another great favourite of the children, the native red squirrel (*Sciuris vulgaris*), lived in the dappled woodland nearby, entrancing them with its beauty and swiftness and a joy for them to watch around its home in the trees.

Both children also shared in the excitement when a magnificent Tay salmon was landed by their father or one of his party. The wild silver salmon, taken from the longest river in Scotland, was yet another subject to sketch as they ate their picnic tea seated with Mrs Potter and her lady companions, whilst they waited for the gentlemen to join them. Sometimes Beatrix and Bertram were permitted to join Mr Potter and his fishermen friends as they got ready to make another cast. Interesting small animals such as voles and shrews lived in the grass of the riverbank and there were frogs and toads to collect in jars, and lizards, all of which were added to their growing collection of pets. And they always kept a sharp look out for that most unusual and ancient fish of the Tay, the lamprey with its large sucker-like mouth, which at first glance seemed to resemble an eel.

Fortunately there was also ample opportunity for Beatrix and Bertram to roam freely on their own. It was the holidays, there were no lessons for them and so when not on outings with their parents they were left, more or less, to their own devices. Together they carefully explored the secret world of hedgerow and ditch, meadow and woodland, often joyfully finding in abundance sweet wild treasure of Scottish raspberry, blaeberry or bramble. Purple-fingered they dawdled homewards, pockets and hands full of the day's wonders.

They decided to make a proper wildlife collection of everything they could find and to record all the details. The list included flowers and plants of every kind, birds (alive and dead) and eggs, together with animals and insects. They were clearly aware as their collection grew that not everything they found and brought home to observe, keep as a pet or dissect if it were dead, would meet with adult approval. If a likely specimen such as an interesting dead bird were found they immediately realised that it would have to be smuggled home for closer inspection at an appropriate time, perhaps when Nurse was busy else-where. Other specimens that would not meet with approval at home were insects of every shape, size and hue. To Beatrix and to Bertram, adult disgust at the sight of a creepie-crawlie was incomprehensible. Ants, beetles, slugs, snails, caterpillars, centipedes, millipedes, spiders and a host of other insects were gradually added to their collection with loving care, and with entrancing Scots names such as Meg-moniefeet (centipede), wabster (spider), and kaleworm (caterpillar) to name but a few, not to mention the joy of hearing and seeing a foggie toddler (bee) overhead, who could resist such wonderful creatures? The Potter children certainly could not.

In the cool shady woods behind the house they found a fascinating array of toadstools and mosses, soft as cushions, which intrigued Beatrix, and sometimes they caught a glimpse of the shy roe deer who lived there. Beatrix remembered these encounters, brief though they were, recalling in beautiful detail a hind she saw running about in the bracken like a rabbit:

> When it went back to feed I crept up nearer, but overdid it at last, and it looked up, with a mouthful of wild sage. The plant hung out like a lettuce-leaf in a rabbit's mouth, and it would munch a moment and then stare, and munch again. When its mouthful was finished, it stretched its neck straight out and uttered a long single bleat, which it repeated presently, pumping up the sound from its flanks to judge by the way it heaved, then it took a header over the bank of fern disappearing into the wood with a twinkle of red and white.[6]

5.3 **Bees and other insects. Beatrix Potter studied and painted many of the wild creatures she discovered on nature rambles.**

Reproduced by kind permission of Frederick Warne & Co.

Sometimes they heard the heart-stopping bark of a fox. On one occasion they even found a dead fox, quietly smuggled it back and skinned and boiled it to see the bone structure. Then, fascinated with all they had discovered during this grisly process, they set about rearticulating the skeleton. Neither of them was in the least squeamish, indeed quite the opposite, as they searched for knowledge. One can guess Nurse McKenzie's reaction however had she discovered them.

In the numerous Highland burns that fed the River Tay they found minnows, sticklebacks and newts and, wonder of wonders, on heather-covered moorland, the occasional adder basking on a warm stone, the bold black zig-zag pattern along its back clear to see. In time they observed how this snake was able to dislocate its jaw to enable it to engulf prey and to slough off its skin, the latter a prize for their collection.

There were plenty of bats roosting in the many outhouses of the estate, most likely common pipistrelle (*Pipistrellus pipistrellus*), the smallest bat in Britain, and Bertram in particular seems to have been especially interested in keeping them as pets. During the summer months female pipistrelles gather in large numbers and perhaps this increased the chance of catching one. The extraordinary flying capability of these little creatures undoubtedly enthralled Beatrix and Bertram. Listening out for the bats' high-pitched calls as they hunted just above their heads and ducking instinctively to avoid a collision, the Potter children enjoyed an aerial performance which never failed to delight them.

At the end of each Dalguise holiday the menagerie of animals, pets and as much of their collection as they could manage without incurring too much adult wrath returned with them to London, Bertram relying entirely on Beatrix to feed and water his specimens, including his bats, once he returned to school. On one occasion, in reply to a letter written to him by Beatrix concerning his pet bats, Bertram wrote:

> I suppose from what you say you will have to let lose [*sic*] the long-eared bats, as they will not eat meat. It is a great pity they are not easier to feed. As for the other, I think it would be almost wrong to let it go, as we might never catch another of that kind again. If he cannot be kept alive as I suppose he can't, you had better kill him, & stuff him as well as you can.[7]

Clearly totally confident in Beatrix's ability and willingness to carry out his instructions Bertram, without sentimentality over the demise of his pet, goes on to remind her to measure the bat before stuffing it, even going into details about how to go about the stuffing to achieve the best results. Bats and other small rodents and insects continued to fascinate Beatrix, as can be seen in the many studies and paintings she made of them during the late 1880s.

Years later when Beatrix was 26 and on holiday with her parents at Birnam, she recorded in her *Journal* an anecdote recounted by the Potters' friend James McDougall, a former Dalguise gamekeeper, on the digestive power of birds, which clearly took her back to Dalguise days of skinning and preserving dead creatures with Bertram for their collection.

> He [McDougall] saw a heron catch four large trout, and shot it while the tail of the last fish still protruded from its mouth. He opened it at once and found that the three first fish were already messed up and unrecognisable, as was also the head of the fourth fish, though its tail had not had time to be swallowed. I can believe a good deal as to the gastric juices of a heron, I once had the misfortune to participate in the skinning of a fine specimen.[8]

Despite Mr and Mrs Potter's fears that Beatrix and Bertram might pick up germs, especially through contact with other children, they clearly did not include pets in this generalisation. As well as her rabbit, Beatrix kept a variety of small animals as pets, which seems not to have unduly concerned her parents. It is conceivable of course that they were not aware of the exact number or type of pets their children kept. Besides Sandy her adored dog and her rabbit, Beatrix cared for her tame hedgehog Mrs Tiggy-winkle whom she fondly described as 'that very stout short person'. Their pets were important to Beatrix and Bertram. They shared their lives with them and when they died, they mourned them. There is a quiet, sheltered corner of the garden at Dalguise House where several miniature, carefully carved headstones to the memory of beloved pets can still be seen today: 'Waddles 23 Sept 1911', 'Lorg Aug 1911' and 'Rags 1923'. A few earlier stones have crumbled away and only traces of them now remain. Perhaps her childhood companion Sandy was finally laid to rest here too.

Summer weather in Scotland could often mean rain and on such days Beatrix and Bertram would work indoors on their paintings. When the air was sultry and the atmosphere heavy with the threat of a summer storm, they eagerly anticipated the first growl of distant thunder as the sky darkened. It was fun for these two amateur scientists to try to count, in a period of say five minutes, the number of lightning flashes which momentarily illuminated the panelled dining room where they sat drawing at the table. Beatrix later recalled, 'it was mostly what Bertram calls *sheep* lightning, though there was some forked'.[9] All her life Beatrix was fascinated by thunderstorms, recording details of many of them in her *Journal*.

However, growing, inquisitive children are also restless and on one occasion, perhaps to get out of a rain shower, they discovered in an outhouse 'a hand press with an agonising squeak'.[10] The fact that it had no ink did not deter them in the least for it appeared to work and was just what they needed to make wood-cuts. They set about making their own ink for it by mixing together soot and colza oil, the latter used in oil lamps. Beatrix recalled the technical difficulties they encountered in trying to attain the correct consistency for printing – 'a sticky black mess, always either too thick or too thin, mixed on a board and applied to the type with a small roller. I can hear it squeak, and always the type wrenched sideways.'[11] They decided to print a few labels for jam jars and offer them to Cook in the hope that their enterprise might attract adult approval. It was not to be – 'the ink was so messy it was confiscated'.[12] It was a salutary lesson not wasted on either of them and in future their more 'messy' investigations were kept well hidden from prying adult eyes.

CHAPTER SIX

'I remember so clearly –
as clearly as the brightness of rich Scotch sunshine...' [1]

HAVING THEIR OWN TRANSPORT with them ensured that the Potters and their guests could travel round the district in comfort whenever they wished to visit acquaintances or view the beautiful Perthshire countryside. As fishing was prohibited on Sundays, a carriage outing was an ideal diversion. Of the many beauty spots close to Dalguise, the famous Hermitage on the Duke of Atholl's estate would have provided an attractive excursion for the Potters and it is almost inconceivable that they would have omitted such a visit during their many holidays at Dalguise. The Hermitage is a place of unforgettable tumbling, rushing, cascading, thundering waterfalls created by the River Braan. The name Braan means 'roaring' and is derived from the Scottish Gaelic word *freamhainn* and an even older root, *bremava*, which means 'noisy' or 'rumbling'. It is a fitting description of a river which surges along beside a wild tree garden of cathedral-like proportions in a woodland setting of exquisite natural beauty. A rustic path leads gently through this idyll of delight to a romantic, ornately decorated summer house with a viewing balcony named Ossian's Hall, after the legendary Celtic bard and warrior, which is poised on the brink of a high rocky promontory. Below it the River Braan plunges in wild fury over a final fall and crashes through a narrow gorge into a seemingly fathomless black pool beyond. When the river is in spate following heavy rain, or fed by melting snow from the hills, the noise, rising through the fine mist of spray, is deafening. A short distance upstream, almost hidden by the undergrowth and lit by dappled sunlight, is a secret place, easily missed, but a place of enchantment to children who discover it. It is Ossian's Cave, a dark little chamber constructed around a group of large boulders and just the place, in the imagination of a child, where Scottish kelpies or dragons or even Ossian himself would choose to live. In fact it was built as an 18th century hermit's folly. The epic poems of Ossian, son of Fingal, had come to public attention in the late 1700s when James Macpherson published them, claiming he had collected and translated them from the Gaelic. Despite their questionable authenticity the poems were extremely popular. The Potters may well have had this literary interest in mind if they did visit The Hermitage during one of their sight-seeing tours from Dalguise and for Beatrix, had she accompanied them, such a visit to the curious old folly would have seemed romantic, exciting and perhaps a touch sinister too. Years later when she wrote

The Tale of Mr. Tod, perhaps Ossian's Cave at The Hermitage, remembered from so long ago, was in her mind.

Following the failure of the Rising of 1745 and the defeat of Bonnie Prince Charlie at Culloden the Jacobite threat seemed to diminish, and this encouraged the Duke of Atholl to proceed with his plan to create The Hermitage. Many old trees that were no longer viable were removed from the banks of the River Braan allowing Scots pine, rowan, oak and other indigenous species to flourish. Each successive Duke added to the planting, including new introductions such as sycamore brought home from abroad by the plant hunters. One of the greatest of these was David Douglas, a native of the small Perthshire town of Scone, who introduced to Scotland from North America the giant fir tree named after him. In 1882, the first year that Dalguise was unavailable for the Potters to lease as usual, Beatrix noted in the garden at Wray Castle in the Lake District, 'Fine specimen of the *Douglas Pine* in garden here, so-called after the gentleman who brought it over.'² The Hermitage remained the exclusive preserve of the Atholl family for many years but by 1860 as its fame spread the Duke wished to show it off to a wider field of suitable visitors and it became fashionable for the upper classes to include the beauty spot in their grand tour. The poet William Wordsworth and his sister Dorothy were among those who came, as did Queen

Victoria during her Tour of 1865. Consequently a visit here may have been included in the itinerary of the Potters and their friends and it is not difficult to imagine the impact such a beautiful place would have made on Beatrix. Besides woodland flowers and bird song, the fine spray from the river created an ideal environment for ferns and mosses to flourish and around the boles of trees there were the 'fine fat fungus'[3] that she mentions in her *Journal* to fascinate her. In due course, ferns, mosses and especially fungi would become central subjects for her art and scientific study.

Rupert Potter's friend, the artist Sir John Everett Millais, perhaps accompanied the Potters to The Hermitage. The River Braan provided the inspiration for many of Millais' paintings.

In a *Journal* entry of 13 October 1892 Beatrix noted, 'It is known now that he painted *St Martin's Summer* just below, near The Hermitage, but he kept it secret

6.2 **The River Braan near Rumbling Bridge, Perthshire.**

at the time.'[4] In fact the setting of the painting closely resembles the area of the River Braan upstream at Rumbling Bridge, also well known to Beatrix, but on the opposite side of the river from where Millais painted *The Sound of Many Waters* in 1876. Beatrix always regarded Millais as one of the most handsome men she ever saw, apart from a small defect in one eye and a mark on his forehead which was mostly hidden by a healthy weather-beaten tan acquired, Beatrix thought, in Scotland from being outdoors fishing, shooting or painting. She had an affectionate regard for the artist despite being 'unmercifully afraid of him as a child... I had a brilliant colour as a little girl, which he used to provoke on purpose.'[5] Millais also recognised Beatrix's artistic talent.

During outings with her parents around Dunkeld the steep wooded heights of Birnam Hill, prominent across the Tay, became a familiar sight to Beatrix. Like children of today who delight to chant well-loved rhymes they have memorised, perhaps Beatrix did too. Familiar as she was with the works of Shakespeare and with Birnam Hill and its surrounding woods, she may have found it fun to repeat, if silently to herself, the famous words uttered by Macbeth:

> I will not be afraid of death and bane
> Till Birnam Forest come to Dunsinane.

Such private games blended perfectly with the happiness Beatrix felt, here on holiday in the place she loved. And it is very likely that she drew additional satisfaction from the fact that she knew the little quotation was from Act V Scene III of the play. When she was 12 years old, Beatrix painted 'the three witches' from *Macbeth*. She did not often include people in her scenes, as figure drawing was not her forte, but in this painting she created a vision of mystery and the supernatural, with the witches gathered round a fire set to one side of a clearing deep in a wood. The bare branches of the trees and the way Beatrix has made the fire the central focus of the painting evoke a sense of eeriness in the floating mist.

Of the many interesting and picturesque expeditions to be enjoyed on foot from Dalguise Beatrix remembered particularly the day she and Bertram walked to Stewartfield in the company of John Bright, their father's friend and fishing guest. From Dalguise House a path leads through dappled woodland towards Glenalbert and on through scented heather towards Stewartfield, 'an old dower house hidden in the fold of the moor, in a stunted wood'.[6] At Mr Bright's request, the old caretaker unlocked the house for them to look inside as Mr Bright particularly wished to examine a small harp reputedly owned by Mary, Queen of Scots. Although by that time Bright was an old man Beatrix never forgot the

BEATRIX POTTER'S SCOTLAND 62

sound of his beautiful, low-pitched voice as he explained the things they saw and found in the empty, forgotten house. Out on the stone terrace they found some strange carved statues which intrigued Beatrix:

> They were stumpy figures about four foot high, presumably mythological – they had very little on. Their workmanship was so crude and unlifelike that nobody with a sense of humour would have found them embarrassing. But the old Scotch gardener abhorred them – "them stukky figgers" he called them... He trained and clipped honeysuckle to encage their nakedness, so that their heads looked out from green mantles of leaves... One goddess used to have a fly-catcher's nest in her bosom every summer, under the honeysuckle flowers.[7]

Mr Bright was good company and the children loved exploring the environs of the old house and garden with him. However there was one puzzle which none of them could solve at the time.

> Beyond the ancient buttressed garden wall were potting sheds, rubbish heaps, and a wet untidy wood, planted with spruce. Some attempt had been made to drain the outskirts of the wood, but in the centre there were strange bankments which even to the eyes of an observant child were mysterious zigzag ridges and ditches, miniature earthworks. Too large to be the work of the wondrous and indefatigable ant; too symmetrical to be excavated by rabbits; too muddy and messy to be made by the fairies (in whom I then believed). On the whole I took them to be a misdirected work of grown-ups, either a small-scale mode of a fortification after the manner of "my Uncle Toby", or a play after the manner of Edie Ochiltree, or by the planters and drainers who had laid out the spruce foundation. These curious little banks and ditches remained a puzzle of childhood and a perplexing memory for many years. I now realise that it was in fact a great rarity and curiosity – an old maze.[8]

Such fascinating and intriguing expeditions were truly wonderful to Beatrix. As she and Bertram returned to Dalguise House with Mr Bright it was exciting to speculate with him as they skipped along at his side, about what they had seen. Perhaps Papa would know? The warm afternoon sunshine and the prospect of a cool glass of freshly made lemonade, served on the lawn, soon occupied the explorers' thoughts.

The spacious gardens of Dalguise House offered many delightful areas in which to relax. There were rustic terraces beside fragrant flowerbeds filled with seasonal blooms. There were charming summer houses in sheltered corners overlooking stone pools filled with limpid water and goldfish. There were wide, manicured lawns laid out on either side of a tumbling burn, which cascaded its crystal-clear way through the garden and delightfully could be crossed at several places by way of tiny stone bridges. Of the many attractive prospects on offer, the favourite gathering place for the family and their guests, at least as far as Beatrix and her father were concerned, was around the beautiful Dalguise Pillar, situated on the lawn not far from the front door of the house. The Dalguise Pillar, an elegant stone column richly carved with spiral fluting and topped by a unicorn, captivated the imagination of both Beatrix and Rupert. It had occupied its place on the Dalguise lawn from about 1850 and may at one time have been an 18th century market cross. Rupert Potter included the Pillar

6.3 **The Dalguise Pillar. Rupert Potter titled this photograph** *After the Salmon Fishing.*

Reproduced by kind permission of Frederick Warne & Co.

in many of his photographs of his family and friends, sometimes including himself in these group studies.

Beatrix greatly admired the elegant Pillar too and she especially loved the myth and magic associated with the symbolic unicorn. Representing status, power, purity and love, by the 15th century the unicorn was part of the heraldic menagerie of the Scottish kings, eventually sharing this with the English lion at the Union of the Crowns in 1603. For Beatrix the fabled beast atop the Pillar was an integral part of Dalguise and needless to say she made a careful, accurate drawing of it. It was as well that she did, for during the next 100 years the Pillar deteriorated and was dismantled with only the base remaining, which no doubt would have saddened Beatrix and her father. But the story of the Dalguise Pillar has a happy ending. During a visit in 1994 to Dalguise House by members of The Beatrix Potter Society the broken fluted columns of the Pillar were discovered lying in the garden, and the unicorn mounted on one of the gate-posts. The Society was instrumental in the restoration of the Pillar: the reference guide in its conservation was none other than the drawing, now in the v & a collection, by a young girl called Beatrix Potter. Today the restored Dalguise Pillar can be seen at the Birnam Institute, next door to the original Birnam Institute and Reading Room, the latter well known to Beatrix when the family stayed in Birnam in 1892. 'Beautiful clear white frost. No end to do. After breakfast went down to the Institute to return books.'9

Beatrix vividly recalled with quiet humour how Sir William Brown, who had posed with her father for a photograph in front of the Dalguise Pillar, would regale the family at dinner with his incredible fishing stories. These he recounted with blow by blow actions and breathless accounts of the struggles he had encountered with the one that eventually got away.

He [Sir William Brown] could catch salmon on hopeless days and in hopeless places – even on the bridge and promenade of his native town... But no salmon that he caught were comparable with the stories of salmon which he had played and lost. Bigger and bigger they waxed after a glass of whiskey[sic]. There was a comical feature of these fishing stories as told over the dinner table; Sir William got hold of every available spoon and fork to map out the plan of the struggle with Leviathan. We had a starched London butler, Mr. Cox, a man excelling in the setting-up of cocked-hat table napkins, immaculate silver and precision cutlery. Behold Mr. Cox hovering in decorous rage while Sir William meanders tablespoons all over the damask... an ever rising agony... "I even turned the fish" (behind the soup tureen more silver forks) "but – he gave a tremend-i-ous wallop..." The salmon parts from the hook, and Mr. Cox sweeps up the spoons and forks and rearranges the dinner table.10

CHAPTER SEVEN

'...the elfin castle...
hidden in the dark glades of Craig Donald Wood.' [1]

WITH EACH SUMMER HOLIDAY spent in Perthshire the love Beatrix felt for Dalguise and the surrounding area deepened. The Potters had become familiar figures to the people of the neighbourhood, some of whom worked on the estate as gamekeepers, gillies or gardeners. Out on nature rambles together Beatrix and Bertram gradually came to know many of the folk that lived nearby and took an interest in the ploys of the two London children, including 'old David Wood, shoemaker and Entomologist... I shall never forget old Mr. Wood coming to Dalguise one hot Monday afternoon,' Beatrix recalled,

> in search of "worms", and producing a present out of his hat of about two dozen buff-tip caterpillars, collected on the road. They ought to have been in a red cotton pocket handkerchief, but they had got loose amongst his venerable grey locks.[2]

There were other people too whose business brought them up to the 'Big House', as it would be known in the neighbourhood. One of these was a local woman called Kitty MacDonald, who made her living by taking in washing. Kitty lived in a tiny cottage at Dalguise and made the short journey on foot up to the house to attend to the laundry of those in residence. Eventually Kitty moved to Kincraigie, a hamlet nestling in the peaceful country between the oak trees of Dalguise and the rowans and silver birch near Kinnaird House. Her homely cottage with its wide views over the valley of the River Tay was situated on the gently sloping hillside and she lived there 'for sixteen years after her Dalguise cottage fell in'.[3] Beatrix remembered Kitty with affection.

> She is a comical, round little old woman, as brown as a berry and wears a multitude of petticoats and a white mutch. [A linen cap worn at the time by women and children.] Her memory goes back for seventy years and I really believe she is prepared to enumerate the articles of her first wash in the year '71

[the year Rupert Potter first took the lease of Dalguise House].[4] The fondness Beatrix felt for her did not fade over their long acquaintance and many years later Beatrix based *The Tale of Mrs. Tiggy-Winkle,* her story about a hedgehog washerwoman, upon her enduring memory of Kitty MacDonald. Beatrix often visited her, delighting in the gentle Scotswoman's wealth of homely stories and reminiscences that often reached far back in history. However, concerning the

'45 Jacobite Rising, Kitty was 'unapproachable on the subject of Prince Charlie'[5] although Beatrix recalled 'she had got something as old as that time, and brought out and unlocked a little tin box and a little parcel, containing a silver brooch'.[6] Kitty was content for Beatrix to handle the little silver brooch fashioned into the shape of two hearts surmounted by a crown, and which Kitty believed had been made by tinkers and used to fasten 'a white kerchief at the throat'.[7]

Travelling people, known locally as tinkers, were a common sight in Perthshire when Beatrix was a child, appearing as itinerant workers at certain times of the year. Keeping themselves to themselves for the most part and speaking the Perthshire cant, a secret language known only to the travelling community, their relationship with the local people was often an uneasy one, neither having any understanding of the other's way of life, and they were usually regarded as poachers when seen near fishing grounds. These tinkers were also known to 'fish' for fresh-water pearls found in the River Tay. For this they used a glass-bottomed tin with a handle to peer into the water and a cleft stick to lift the mussel shells containing, they hoped, the prized pearls.

Beatrix remembered old Dr Irving of Pitlochry describing how 'he had introduced safety pins to the civilised world'[8] based on a crude garment fastener used by tinkers in the district. It was just the sort of story that intrigued Beatrix and appealed to her scientific, enquiring mind.

> He saw a gypsy wife with her plaid fastened with an odd twist of wire, and thinking it ingenious, took it as a pattern to the Museum in Dunkeld. I remember his lamenting that he had not taken out a patent.[9]

Beatrix guessed that the safety pin, now universally used in modern life, probably dated from very early times as a means of fastening garments. The Romans, after all, fastened their togas with a double brooch arrangement resembling a large chain cuff-link although it was also true to say that brooches and buckles were of Celtic and Greek origin too. 'I suppose,' she noted, 'it was the application of the principle to wire which was a new departure. How old is wire? The spirit of enquiry leads up a lane which hath no ending.'[10] That 'spirit of enquiry' stayed with Beatrix Potter all her life.

There were occasional days during the holidays when the family's individual interests predominated, Rupert Potter accompanied by Sir John Millais choosing for a change to cast a fly on a different beat of the Tay or perhaps a day on the hill grouse shooting with McIntosh the Dalguise gamekeeper. If the day were fine Mrs Potter and Lady Millais departed after lunch to enjoy a drive in the

7.1 **Charlie McIntosh, 'the Perthshire Naturalist' and postman.**

Reproduced by kind permission of Perth Museum and Art Gallery, Perth and Kinross Council, Scotland.

phaeton, combining their tour with a visit to friends in Dunkeld. Sometimes 'the nursery authorities' were otherwise engaged and occasionally even Bertram was busy about his own affairs. Then, for Beatrix, it was wonderful to sit undisturbed in a sunny upstairs window seat of Dalguise House to daydream and sketch in peace. From this high eyrie she could also gaze out over the garden and the treetops to the hills beyond. It was the perfect place to relax and relish being back at her beloved Dalguise. From her excellent vantage point Beatrix could casually note the comings and goings of any visitors approaching the house by the main driveway. One such person was the familiar figure of the local postman Charles McIntosh, known to everyone including Beatrix as Charlie, making his way up the drive to deliver letters as part of his 16-mile round, a journey he made on foot every day regardless of weather. 'I forget how many thousand miles he walked,' Beatrix later wrote, 'some mathematical person reckoned it up.'[11] It seemed to Beatrix that Charlie always appeared to be looking down at his boots as he strode steadily along. Some years later she recalled how when she was a child it had been 'an amusement' after Charlie had delivered the mail and departed on his way 'to hop from puddle to puddle on the strides of Charlie's hob-nailed boots'.[12] In a letter written over 30 years later to Henry Coates of Perth, author of *A Perthshire Naturalist*, a biography of Charles McIntosh, Beatrix had written:

> I can remember him [Charlie] since July, 1870, swinging up the avenue, with long strides and head down, and a very small child [Beatrix herself], sent to "get the letters", waiting under a copper beech. Perhaps I remember this because, on that first occasion, I ran away – I don't know which one of us was shyest![13]

As she grew older Beatrix learned there was purpose in Charlie's seemingly peculiar gait. He was keeping an alert lookout for specimens, for he had a particular interest in fungi, ferns and mosses, and indeed was acknowledged as something of an expert.

'His successor has a tricycle:' Beatrix wrote in 1892 when Charlie had retired,

> it will save his legs, but modern habits and machines are not calculated to bring out individuality or the study of Natural History. Country postmen, at all events in Scotland, are almost always men of intelligence with some special study. Probably the result of much solitary thinking and observation.[14]

It was an observation she could easily have made of herself.

Beatrix was 16 as another thoroughly satisfactory holiday in Perthshire came to an end and the family prepared to return to London. The year was wearing on. Dazzling autumn sunshine slanted low through trees burnished gold.

Crisp leaves drifted to the ground in the still air and there was often a nip of frost in the mornings now. For Beatrix, it was hard to be leaving the place she loved most in the world.

> I remember every stone, every tree, the scent of the heather, the music sweetest mortal ears can hear, the murmuring of the wind through the fir trees. Even when the thunder growled in the distance, and the wind swept up the valley in fitful gusts, oh, it was always beautiful, home sweet home.[15]

Spot, her beloved spaniel dog, in the local parlance 'belonged to Dalguise', meaning he originated from Dalguise, and Beatrix was devoted to him. It was a consolation that as they prepared to leave she and Spot could at least look forward to returning 'home' to Dalguise next year. Another consolation for Beatrix was that Papa had taken numerous photographs to remind them all of Perthshire.

Dalguise House felt, to Beatrix at any rate, as though it *was* her family home. In fact, by adding together each annual three-month period over the eleven consecutive years that Rupert Potter leased the house, the Potters were in residence for almost three years of the eleven.

The Laird of Dalguise was one John Steuart, born in 1798 and said to be one of the last descendants of King Robert II of Scotland (1316–90). Steuart had left Dalguise for Capetown in South Africa, where he became a judge and Master of the Supreme Court, although in so doing he did not give up his Scottish estate, which is why Rupert Potter was able to take the Dalguise House lease year after year. It was an admirable arrangement all round and seemed set to continue for the foreseeable future. Following the Potters' holiday of 1881, however, Rupert was advised that the Dalguise rent had been increased to £450, a sum he regarded as exorbitant. He was now faced with a stark choice. If he wished to continue the following year at their beloved Dalguise, he would have to pay the increased rent or look elsewhere.

In November of 1881 Beatrix began her *Journal*. In the spring of the following year she recorded on 20 April that her parents had decided to travel to Scotland, presumably to review the lease situation for themselves before making a decision. 'Papa, mamma and Elizabeth [their maid] went to Dalguise. Seems to me we've been nicely done.'[16] One week later Elizabeth, with Spot, arrived back in London a day ahead of her employers. The Potters would *not* be returning to Dalguise after all. On the exact date the lease expired Beatrix wrote in her *Journal*, 'Dalguise lease out on 11th May – no one yet taken it, though several been considering,' adding, 'Probably stopped by the ridiculous rent, £450.'[17] What Beatrix did not know was that John Steuart had died in Cape Colony on

7.2 **Beatrix Potter with her parents, her brother Bertram, and Spot the family dog at Dalguise.**

Reproduced by kind permission of The Beatrix Potter Society. Photograph by Rupert Potter.

28 December 1881. His estate had passed to his grandson Charles H. Durrant Steuart, who now occupied Dalguise House himself; as the new Laird, he had terminated Rupert Potter's lease. The Potters' Dalguise idyll, it seemed, had come to an end. Beatrix's *Journal* of late autumn and winter 1881 is silent on the subject of Dalguise.

For the summer of 1882 her father made other arrangements for the family holiday, as Beatrix briefly notes in her *Journal*, 'Monday, July 10th – Papa took Wray Castle.'[18] In choosing Wray Castle, a large house in the style of a mock Norman castle, situated on the west side of Windermere in the English Lake District, Rupert Potter had broken the long Potter tradition of holidays in Scotland. Although pleased enough with Wray Castle, the Potters still hankered it seems for the old days in Perthshire and in May 1884 it seemed as though a return to

Dalguise might be a possibility. This was unexpected and troubling news for Beatrix and for the first time since the day she packed up her paintings and her pressed flowers, fossils and fungi, her little pets in their travelling boxes, and left Dalguise with its precious bright memories, her *Journal* reveals the extent of her paradise lost.

I feel an extraordinary dislike to this idea, a childish dislike, but the memory of that home is the only bit of childhood I have left. It was not perfectly happy, childhood's sorrows are sharp while they last, but they are like April showers serving to freshen the fields and make the sunshine brighter than before.

We watch the gentle rain on the mown grass in April, and feel a quiet peace and beauty. We feel and hear the roaring storm of November, and find the peace gone, the beauty become wild and strange. Then as we struggle on, the thoughts of that peaceful past time of childhood comes to us like soft music and a blissful vision through the snow. We do not wish we were back in it, unless we are daily broken down, for the very good reason that it is impossible for us to be so, but it keeps one up, and there is a vague feeling that one day there will again be rest.

The place is changed now, and many familiar faces are gone, but the greatest change is in myself. I was a child then, I had no idea what the world would be like...

Half believing the picturesque superstitions of the district, seeing my own fancies so clearly that they became true to me, I lived in a separate world. Then just as childhood was beginning to shake, we had to go, my first great sorrow. I do not wish to have to repeat it, it has been a terrible time since, and the future is dark and uncertain, let me keep the past. The old plum tree is fallen, the trees are felled, the black river is an open hollow, the elfin castle is no longer hidden in the dark glades of Craig Donald Wood....

I could not see it in the same way now, I would rather remember it with the sun sinking, showing, behind the mountains, the purple shadows creeping down the ravines into the valley to meet the white mist rising from the river. Then, an hour or two later, the great harvest-moon rose over the hills, the fairies came out to dance on the smooth turf, the night-jar's eerie cry was heard, the hooting of the owls, the bat flitted round the house, roe-deer's bark sounded from the dark woods, and faint in the distance, then nearer and nearer came the strange wild music of the summer breeze.[19]

CHAPTER EIGHT

'How fast the swifts fly here, how clearly the birds sing, how long the twilight lasts!' [1]

IT WAS 11 YEARS before the Potters spent another summer holiday in Perthshire. Beatrix was almost three months away from her 17th birthday but feeling far from joyful when she confided to her Journal,

> I am up one day and down another. Have been a long way down today, and now my head feels empty and I am nothing particular. Will things never settle? Is this being grown-up? If I could have seen my mind as it is now, when I left Dalguise I should not have known it. [2]

To make matters worse a new governess seemed to be a possibility, and although Beatrix was confident that her father would not force her to accept a new governess against her wishes she was dismayed that any revised timetable in the schoolroom was bound to mean less time for painting. 'I can't settle to any thing but my painting, I lost my patience over everything else.'[3] The new governess was Miss Annie Carter, later to become Mrs Moore.

In May 1884, however, Beatrix accompanied her parents on a brief visit to Edinburgh. The exciting prospect of seeing Scotland's capital, with all its historic and romantic associations, for herself filled Beatrix with delight, and she promised herself that she would 'write voluminously'[4] about the city she had read of so often and which was one of the places she wished most to see. There was, however, an aspect of the Edinburgh trip which she dreaded: 'there is the chance of going on to Dunkeld, O Home, I cannot bear to see it again. How times and I have changed!'[5] There had been reports of changes in the Dalguise area since the Potters' last visit there and not apparently for the better. 'Don't know why papa is so anxious to go,' Beatrix wrote, 'I don't want to at all.'[6] But Rupert Potter had made up his mind and the family, minus Bertram who was at school, arrived at the Birnam Hotel, run by Mr Pople, on 26 May. Despite her private reservations, arrival at the comfortable, welcoming hotel was a delight.

May is a beautiful month in the Highlands as new growth, colour and bird-song awaken in the hills and glens after a long winter and sometimes a cold spring. Beatrix was keen to explore her immediate surroundings and after tea walked down to the banks of the River Tay. As of old, she was once more inspired. 'The grass is greener, the flowers thicker and finer,' she wrote. 'It is fancy, but everything seems so much more pleasant here. The sun is warmer and air sharper.' Perhaps the reports they had heard about decline in the area had been exaggerated after all. It was a cheering thought as she surveyed the beauty of the scene around her on such a lovely evening.

> Man may spoil a great deal, but he cannot change the everlasting hills, or the mighty river, whose golden waters still flow on at the same measured pace, mysterious, irresistible. There are few more beautiful and wonderful things than a great river. I have seen nothing like it since I left; down to the smell of the pebbles on the shore, it may be drainage, but it brings back pleasant memories.[7]

Beatrix had prepared herself for a changed countryside. Now, as she strolled back to the hotel in the soft Highland gloaming, it seemed there might be room for hope after all. They were to visit Dalguise the following day. 'I remember *Home* clearer and clearer, I seem to have left it but yesterday. Will it be much changed?' she wondered. As ever though, as she returned to the hotel, her attention focused on the natural scene around her. 'How fast the swifts fly here, how clearly the birds sing, how long the twilight lasts!'[8]

Her cautious optimism was tested when she accompanied her parents to Dalguise the next day. As they drove along, their hired carriage drawn by a grey horse, but not, alas, by their own Berry or Snowdrops, Beatrix noted small changes here and there. The bridge at Inver had been re-built and there were some new railings on the Duke of Atholl's land. Trees she remembered as saplings had grown while others had fallen or died, but on the whole she was able to say that the place had not changed that much. 'It is home,'[9] she wrote. But the homecoming was not the happy, eager journey of the old days. Dalguise estate looked run down and neglected. She was perplexed to see a sawmill opposite the house and an ugly telegraph wire spoiled the driveway, and inevitably some of the old people she remembered had died and others gone away. Whether it was true for Beatrix to claim that 'the curse of drink is heavy on the land'[10] and the demise of the estate inevitable is not known. For Beatrix, it could never be the same again. The golden years of Dalguise were over and she preferred to remember it as it had once been.

Two months later, at home again in London, Beatrix briefly reflected in her *Journal*,

> I am eighteen today. How time does go. I feel as if I had been going on such a time. How must grandmamma feel – What funny notions of life I used to have as a child! I often thought of the time when I should be eighteen – it's a queer business.[11]

It seemed as though she had finally drawn a line under her Dalguise childhood.

8.1 **Looking south east down the River Tay from Telford's bridge at Dunkeld.**

Beatrix had grown into a young woman. From the nursery at No. 2 Bolton Gardens she continued to draw and paint and to look after her beloved pets as usual, quietly mourning the passing of Xarifa her pet dormouse in the winter of 1887. 'I wonder,' she reflected sadly,

> if ever another dormouse had so many acquaintances, Mr. Bright, Mr. J. Millais, and Mr. Leigh Smith had admired and stroked her, amongst others. I think she was in many respects the sweetest little animal I ever knew.[12]

Another dear old friend, William Gaskell, had passed away too. 'There has always been a deep child-like affection between him and me,'[13] she wrote. 'The memory of it is one of the past lights bound up with the old home.'[14] Dalguise was ever fresh in her mind. The Potters sent flowers but did not attend

Gaskell's funeral, which was taking place at Knutsford. He was, nevertheless, very much in Beatrix's thoughts.

> Shall I really never see him again? But he is gone with almost every other, home is gone for me, the little girl does not bound about now, and live in fairyland, and occasionally wonder in a curious, carefree manner, as of something not concerning her nature, what life means, and whether she shall ever feel sorrow. It is all gone, and he is resting quietly with our fathers. I have begun the dark journey of life. Will it go on as darkly as it has begun? Oh that I might go through life as blamelessly as he![15]

Although Beatrix continued to live upstairs in the schoolroom the difference now was that she had much more contact with her parents and had become their young adult companion. In their company Beatrix visited sale rooms to look at furniture and china. 'Mamma ended in buying a Chippendale clock, fourteen guineas. Cheap I think.'[16] She went to the theatre, visited relatives and as always went on holiday with her parents. She frequently accompanied her father to art galleries and exhibitions and was dismayed to see more and more of the Old Masters going abroad. Although her first love was drawing and painting the natural world, she was also increasingly interested in practical photography, learning much from her father who had become accomplished in this new art form. When Sir John Millais was commissioned to paint the portrait of the Prime Minister, William Gladstone, Millais had asked Rupert Potter to assist him by photographing his distinguished sitter. In her *Journal*, Beatrix recorded how Gladstone had discussed non-technical aspects of photography with her father and asked for his opinion as to whether it would ever be possible to photograph in colour.

Many of her father's friends were politicians and Beatrix found politics absorbing, especially coverage of the General Election of 1886. She regularly read the newspapers and like her beloved grandmother Potter, Beatrix loved anecdotes. If her grandmother's anecdotes were recounted from events in her own long life, Beatrix sometimes gleaned hers from newspaper reports and frequently attempted to capture dialect in her *Journal*. One humorous story concerned a franchise demonstration in Scotland.

> A country man who had been toiling under a large banner inscribed *Down with the Peers*, was asked what he knew about the matter; he replied "he didna ken muckle, but he wished Peers was doon, and the same price as aiples".[17]

Perhaps the Scots accent reconnected her with Perthshire? Perhaps a newspaper report of the death of Cluny McPherson, grandson of the clan chief who had lost all in his support for Bonnie Prince Charlie and the doomed Jacobite cause, did too?

A highlight of 1884 was the purchase of a little carriage, and to pull it a 16-year-old pony called Bobby, described by Beatrix as 'the neatest daisy-cropper I ever saw'.[18] She quickly learned to drive the pony and trap whilst on holiday at Bush Hall in Hertfordshire, a property owned by Lord Salisbury, which her father had leased for the summer of 1884. It was a useful skill to acquire, for Beatrix was able to utilise it to the full several years later when, once more, the Potters returned to Perthshire for their summer holiday. For the meantime short holiday breaks continued at south coast resorts and with the Lake District increasingly favoured for the summer, Rupert Potter rented Lingholm near Keswick for the first time in 1885 as their holiday base. Although Lingholm was beautifully situated, one wonders if thoughts of Perthshire were in her mind when Beatrix wrote 'I wish we had a settled home!'[19]

Inevitably, as she grew older and as an only daughter, Beatrix became much involved in family matters. The winter of 1887 had been particularly trying for the whole family. Bertram, unhappy at boarding school where he was not doing particularly well anyway, contracted pleurisy. Helen Potter was shocked to receive a telegram containing the news that her brother, William Leech, had died suddenly and unexpectedly of inflammation of the lungs. Beatrix privately noted however that her uncle's drinking habits had contributed not a little to his demise. Grandmama Potter had also been very ill the previous summer whilst in London and the family had therefore decided to spend that holiday at Camfield Place, Grandmama Potter's Hertfordshire home, taking their own servants with them to prepare in advance for Grandmama's return there. The holiday had been something of a nightmare as the housekeeper employed to look after Camfield during Grandmama Potter's absence had allowed the place to get into a filthy condition. Far from being the 'palatial residence'[20] Beatrix remembered from childhood, open drains and other potential hazards to health were discovered: 'Why no one ever had a fever, passes me,'[21] Beatrix wrote, as the entire household and servants endeavoured to put things to rights, hindered at first by incompetent workmen and plumbers.

Bertram recovered from pleurisy but Mr and Mrs Potter continued to be perplexed over the question of what to do about school arrangements for him. Prior to this the family's much-needed spring holiday to Grange-over-Sands had been cut short and an immediate return to London undertaken when Beatrix herself had become seriously ill 'with something uncommonly like rheumatic fever'[22], from which she did not fully recover until the summer, much to the relief of her frantic parents. Bertram was eventually settled back into his old Eastbourne school and Beatrix and her parents at last resumed life more or less as before. Following a visit to Christie's the auctioneers the following spring, to view a collection of paintings, Beatrix commented in her *Journal* that they had been 'selected with admirable taste, no rubbish and nothing vulgar'.[23] The large number of animal paintings, particularly of red deer, clearly interested her and she pondered the skill of painters who specialised in this subject. With the eye of a naturalist and thinking of the many times she herself had inspected red deer shot on the Perthshire hills by her father's shooting parties, she was able to make particular observations with a certain authority as to the anatomical accuracy, or otherwise, displayed by these artists.

> To any person who has handled a dead deer, especially a few hours after it has been shot, when rigid stiffening has to some extent supplied the tense resistance of life, the prevailing impression is of the wooden impracticability of the wiry legs. It is far more like an arrangement of walking-sticks than steaks.[24]

And in a further shrewd comment about the skill of English artists painting deer in the style of Landseer, Beatrix observed,

> [They] are so absorbed by the grace and suppleness of hoofed animals' legs, that they rather lose sight of the circumstances that the legs are primarily wooden pegs to support the body, the balanced springs superadded to give ease in motion.[25]

A further point Beatrix was able to make of many animal paintings she viewed at galleries in general was the 'over-doing of sleekness'[26], a fair comment based on her own minutely observed and accurately drawn animals.

At the age of 24 Beatrix appeared to have few friends of her own age until a letter of February 1890 in her *Journal* introduced 'Esther'[27]. Beatrix had been to the Winter Exhibition at the Royal Academy and was writing afterwards to Esther to tell her all about it and, like most young women in their early 20s, comment upon the latest fashions. 'Esther' is however believed to have been an imaginary friend inspired by the diary of Fanny Burney, whom Beatrix greatly admired. Later that year Beatrix wrote again to 'Esther' through the pages of her *Journal* with news on a much more significant subject. After several rejections by other publishers, the firm of Hildesheimer & Faulkner had accepted drawings Beatrix had submitted to them as possible Christmas cards, and had paid her £6. Beatrix was delighted and celebrated.

My first act was to give Bounce (what an investment that rabbit has been in spite of the hutches), a cupful of hemp seeds [Benjamin Bouncer, her pet rabbit had been her model for the designs], the consequence being that when I wanted to draw him next morning he was partially intoxicated and wholly unmanageable.[28]

It was the first of her work to be published.

In June 1891 Beatrix had the pleasure of meeting at Putney Park, London, Mrs Hugh Blackburn, the author of *Birds from Nature*, the book Beatrix had received with such dancing delight from her parents for her tenth birthday all those years ago at Dalguise. Beatrix found Mrs Blackburn a delightful person, and later recorded full details in her *Journal* of their meeting including particulars of the admired author's appearance and conversation. Nor did Beatrix omit to mention 'her love of nature expressed in sweet homely Scotch made one think of Burns'[29] and her description of 'her beautiful Argyllshire home, where the mild Trade Wind blows all winter, and "the sea is never *cauld*"'.[30]

CHAPTER NINE

*'I think myself that a house that is too small is more comfortable
than one a great deal too large.'* [1]

THE HEATHER-CLAD HILLS of Perthshire are purple-hued and honey-scented by the end of July. Red deer stags take their ease in remote corries on the high tops, the golden eagle circles majestically, grouse burst forth from the shimmering heather calling 'go back, go back, go back'. In glen and garden alike the air is fragrant with flowers. Summer has reached its high point. On 27 July 1892 Beatrix stepped down from the train at Birnam station at the start of her summer holiday. The following day she would be 26.

The journey to Perthshire from King's Cross in London had for Beatrix been one of mixed feelings and nostalgia this time. Apart from the many familiar landmarks she always anticipated seeing from the train as it bustled northwards, Beatrix also remembered the numerous small things from previous journeys, like the little hedgehog she had once noticed feasting on spring cabbages in the tiny garden at Cockburnspath station. She did not see it this time but smiled to herself as she recalled 'the business-like manner'[2] in which the little creature had hurried from cabbage to cabbage taking a mouthful from each in the process. The journey was also tinged with sadness. Grandmama Potter had passed away the previous autumn leaving a gap which for Beatrix could not be filled. Also Spot, her beloved spaniel, had died that April and for the first time in 10 years the family were travelling without him. Beatrix missed his joyfulness and bounding enthusiasm, as he got under everyone's feet in his eagerness not to be left behind. Eventually, properly installed in his place in front of the luggage he 'smiled benignly between his curls'.[3]

Another beloved animal who *was* travelling with Beatrix to Scotland however was her pet rabbit, Benjamin Bunny. As the train neared Dunbar station Beatrix took him out of his travelling basket to check that all was well and despite being a seasoned traveller poor Benjamin took fright and 'bit the family'.[4] Twelve hours after leaving King's Cross the Potters arrived at Perth station where they had breakfast and bought the morning papers, *The Scotsman* instead of *The Times* now they were back in Perthshire. The 'caustic comments'[5] in *The Scotsman* on the ongoing strike at the steelworks of the Scots-born millionaire Andrew Carnegie prompted Beatrix to reflect 'Scotch papers are refreshingly acrimonious and spiteful provided you agree with them... They make *The Times* leaders appear ponderous in comparison.'[6] Despite improvements to Perth

9.1 **Beatrix Potter with her dog, Spot.**

Reproduced by kind permission of
The Beatrix Potter Society.
Photograph by Rupert Potter.

station since their last visit however, Beatrix was unimpressed with poor service in the first-class restaurant. It was with some relief, therefore, that the Potters finally reached Birnam station and journey's end at 8 p.m.

For the summer holiday of 1892 Rupert Potter had taken the lease on Heath Park, a modest villa a little over 30 years old, which had been built by a local man who had subsequently made his money abroad and settled there permanently. Standing prominently in its one-acre garden with views over Birnam station and the romantic Highland countryside beyond it, Heath Park was as different from Dalguise House as can be imagined. Heath Park was also very much smaller than Dalguise House. Although Rupert Potter was well aware of this when he committed to the lease, the letting agent being none other than the Potters' old friend Mr Kinnaird, the Birnam station-master, nevertheless a slight doubt arose and preyed on Rupert's mind. Would Heath Park be large enough to comfortably accommodate them all? Before leaving London, therefore, he had made reservations for the family at the Birnam Hotel for the first night of their holiday – just in case.

The hotel had changed hands since the Potters' last visit and was now managed by a Mr Cesari. Beatrix noted wryly that this gentleman claimed descent from Julius Caesar and displayed a plaster bust of the Roman general in the corridor of the hotel. She also noted that in the opinion of some patrons, the famous Birnam Hotel under Mr Cesari's management was not quite so comfortable as in former times when Mr and Mrs Pople were the owners. Thinking back perhaps to that idyllic evening eight years earlier when she had stayed there with her parents, Beatrix described the hotel now as 'less homely'[7] than hitherto. Certainly, in John Pople's time, the Birnam's reputation for excellence was known far and wide, with every person of quality, nobility and gentry alike staying there, the ladies accompanied by their own maids, the gentlemen by their own valets. With large stables attached, the hotel also held the posting business for the north. Every morning by 4 a.m. John Pople was up and about, directing his staff in every aspect of the day's work in the hotel and the stables. Nothing was overlooked that might inconvenience his guests or jeopardize the hotel's reputation. In the evening Mr Pople was again present, standing by the door of the dining room at 7.30 p.m. to welcome his guests, bowing to each in turn. The dining room, decorated in Scottish baronial style, the very height of fashion at that time, was situated at the top of stairs and so enabled each pair of guests to make a grand entrance. When all were ushered in, John Pople retired to bed with strict instructions that he was not to be disturbed until morning. Such a well-run

9.2 **The Birnam Hotel.**

establishment was exactly what the Potters liked and expected, and despite the change of ownership the Birnam Hotel was as popular as ever. It was fortunate, therefore, that Rupert Potter had reserved rooms in advance as it was very busy. From her chair in the dining room Beatrix even observed improvements in some of the staff, 'the *boots* had learnt to pour coffee from a height without scalding the recipient, though still rather liable to direct one of the twin streams into the hot-milk jug'.[8]

The Potters moved into Heath Park the following day. The ground upon which the house was built had once been part of the heathery hillside above it and from this topography the house took its name, for in Scots a park is a grassy or in this case a heathery enclosure near or round a house. Beatrix seems to have been unaware of this meaning and was therefore puzzled by the terminology 'park', which seemed to suggest something rather grand, and recorded in her *Journal* 'in spite of its fine name [Heath Park] is a Villa'.[9] Although well built, Heath Park looked slightly shabby owing to lack of regular maintenance and an absentee owner. Similarly the garden, with no regular gardener employed to look after it, had become overgrown and neglected. There were however, as Beatrix observed when she walked round it, large quantities of green gooseberries for the picking although rabbits had long since gnawed every scrap of bark from the other fruit trees. The gooseberries soon became a favourite fruit of Benjamin Bunny who stood on his back legs to eat the succulent green orbs hanging from the bushes. There were also potatoes in the garden, perhaps planted to improve the ground fertility at one time, but which had long since gone to seed. Despite this they continued to give a yield, 'only the size of walnuts: but sweet'.[10] Heath Park held another unexpected surprise that greatly amused Beatrix. From the time of their arrival and during their entire stay, her father became an enthusiastic train spotter. 'Situated,' Beatrix recalled, 'at what an auctioneer's clerk would call "a convenient remove" from the Station',[11] the view down to the station from the edge of the Heath Park garden was excellent for the purpose of train spotting, having the dual attributes of being elevated, yet secluded from public view. 'The trains prove to be a source of constant amusement,' Beatrix wrote. 'Papa is constantly running out, and looks out of the bedroom window in the night.'[12] She also shared her father's appreciation of the splendid locomotives that shook station platforms and thundered through the countryside. 'Some people can see no sentiment or beauty in a railway, simply a monstrosity and a matter of dividends. To my mind,' she wrote, her usual pragmatism mingled with the eye and sentiment of an artist,

> there is scarcely a more splendid beast in the world than a large Locomotive: if it loses something of mystery through being the work of man, it surely gains in a corresponding degree the pride of possession. I cannot imagine a finer sight than the Express, with two engines, rushing down this incline at the edge of dusk.[13]

Despite its proximity to the railway station however, Heath Park was peacefully situated and screened by trees from the neighbours. These turned out to be

'English lodgers'[14] on one side and on the other a Mr McInroy, an elderly gentleman who wore the kilt, with his wife, their five daughters, two sons who seemed to do nothing except idle their time away, and their pet terrier dog. Although the trees ensured visual privacy between the gardens it was impossible for the Potters not to overhear Mr McInroy in the next garden, frequently and crossly expressing his dissatisfaction with one or other of his family who had incurred his wrath, assuring the individual involved that he would '"never ask you to do anything again as long as I live".'[15] Furthermore the McInroys seemed inexplicably reluctant to make the acquaintance of their new London neighbours. This fact amused Beatrix since 'we ourselves are most standoffish and unsociable amongst promiscuous neighbours, "wouldn't speak to them for words", so that this turn of the tables is an acceptable joke'.[16] From time to time, when she was in the village, Beatrix encountered the elder of the two McInroy sons, a rather surly individual, making his way to or returning from the Recreation Ground where he seemed to spend his day. Although dressed in white flannels and carrying a tennis racquet he did not play, but instead passed idle days there doing nothing. Mrs Potter, also by chance, met the reluctant Mrs McInroy when shopping at the greengrocers' in Birnam. The latter, a tall old lady wearing a crinoline and ringlets, responded to the greeting in alarmed confusion and with an expression resembling 'that of a startled hen'[17], as Mrs Potter described it later. The explanation for the McInroys' extraordinary avoidance tactics towards their neighbours, and other local people, appeared to be common knowledge. Old Mr McInroy had, it seemed, as Beatrix recorded in her *Journal*, 'become insolvent, under Trust'[18], a state of affairs which his wife and family clearly felt to be something of a social stigma.

As Mr and Mrs Potter and the rest of the household settled into their new surroundings, they were thankful that while the house was large enough and certainly quite roomy after all it could hardly be described as spacious. For her part, Beatrix was content to note as she finished her own unpacking, 'I think myself that a house that is too small is more comfortable than one a great deal too large.'[19] The stables were tiny and some manoeuvring was required before the Potters' horses were safely installed. A couple of days later Aunt Clara (Rupert's sister) and her friend Miss Gentile arrived as planned by train from London, with reservations at the Birnam Hotel. It was quite possible too that the Potters' friend Sir John Millais and his family would visit them at some point during the holiday. Millais, who knew the area well, had rented nearby Birnam Hall for ten years until 1891 for, like the Potters, the Millais family loved to holiday in Perthshire. Then there were the many old friends and places in the district the Potters themselves intended to visit. The holiday had begun.

The first few days following their arrival in Birnam had proved quite hectic, especially for Beatrix as she endeavoured to establish her parents at Heath Park for the duration of their holiday. Beatrix, although in the prime of life herself, had increasingly become indispensable in her parents' lives, and they relied heavily upon her always being there for them. Indeed they expected it. For her part Beatrix accepted her role of attentive daughter and companion to them as her duty. Even so she was always aware of the need to have a little private time of her own whenever she could and so, with the household finally settled, she stepped at last into the quiet lane behind Heath Park to explore her immediate surroundings. She found spires of rosebay willow-herb and patches of heather beside back garden walls where toadflax and hart's tongue fern flourished in cracks in the crumbled stonework. Wild roses and honeysuckle, scrambling beside a row of old cottages, deliciously scented the evening air. Miss Hutton's black cat, sitting on the path beside a clump of thistles, licked a dainty paw and twitched its tail. The stony path continued to the splashing Inchewan Burn that tumbled nearby in numerous delightful cascades, down the hill, beside the path to the village a short walk away. A little brown-and-white bird, a dipper, perched and bobbed on a half-submerged boulder midstream before diving beneath the water to surface, perch and bob again, on another prominent stone further up the burn. Unseen wood pigeons crooned from the dark recesses of summer foliage. Honey bees laboured late. It was all part of the Perthshire scene Beatrix loved. Last but not least as she stood by the gate at the back of Heath Park, the familiar sight of little Birnam Hill rose steeply behind.

The Potters were not the only visitors arriving in Birnam that July of 1892. Strains of bagpipe music could be heard drifting across the village to the hills from the golf course where some 700 Perthshire Volunteers of the Black Watch Highland Regiment were camped. From the jute mills of Dundee, too, workers were escaping the grime of the city for their week of holiday freedom and breath of fresh air in the Birnam countryside. It appeared that in common with Rupert Potter many of the factory workers were fascinated by the arrival and departure of the trains and spent much of their holiday, as Beatrix observed, 'at the Station, instead of in the woods'.[20]

By the end of their first week in Birnam the Potters were at last comfortably settled at Heath Park. With Aunt Clara and Miss Gentile joining them for one week there was plenty of conversation for the ladies and the prospect of fishing

9.3 **Birnam railway station**

for Bertram and his father. Beatrix was busy, too, 'finishing a drawing of a Jackdaw for Nister & Co.', a German firm of fine art colour printers with an office in London, who had bought a few of her drawings, 'for which, by the way, they have not paid'.[21] By chance a tame jackdaw began visiting Heath Park at this time, a handy reference for Beatrix, and was soon identified as the property of Miss Hutton and her elderly brother Willy, the local joiner, who lived in the cottages behind Heath Park. Miss Hutton also owned a large black cat which frequently wandered into Heath Park garden and which, to her dismay, Beatrix had seen standing on its hind legs looking into the rabbit hutch. The same cat had brought home three wild rabbits it had killed. It was little wonder that Beatrix kept a sharp look out for this and numerous other felines that lived in the vicinity, and decided for safety to walk Benjamin about the garden on a leather lead. Benjamin was rather accident prone anyway; Beatrix recalled how he had once fallen head-first into an aquarium filled with water and, as he was unable to climb out on his own, sat there 'pretending to eat a piece of string'. Beatrix rather admired his panache. 'Nothing like putting a face upon circumstances,'[22] she wrote in her Journal. On one Heath Park garden outing with Beatrix, Benjamin met a small, rather scruffy wild rabbit at the edge of the cabbage patch who was eager to make his acquaintance. Enchanted, Beatrix watched as the tiny stranger, a female, cautiously approached Benjamin making little grunting noises, but to no avail. The handsome but 'stupid' Benjamin continued to eat the cabbage leaves, ignoring the visitor until he met her face to face round one of the cabbage plants and, perhaps mistaking her for Miss Hutton's cat, immediately bolted in fright.

The garden was also a good place in which to sketch and write picture-letters to the Moore children and to keep up her regular correspondence with their mother and Miss Hammond. The short walk with her letters down the hill to Birnam post-office from Heath Park was one Beatrix enjoyed, providing she was not in a hurry when she got there. The post master, presiding behind the counter, conducted business at an unhurried pace from which he would not be deflected. Beatrix recorded a wonderful word picture of the scene.

> He is a fat, hunched old fellow, with little piggy eyes, a thick voice and wears a smoking-cap with a yellow tassel, and he has immense hands with which he slowly fumbles about for the stamps, which he keeps amongst the stationery in empty writing-paper boxes. He puts on wrong postage "shall we say tuppence?(!)" and will sauce anybody who is unprovided with small change; he wants reporting.[23]

Rupert Potter also busied himself with his photographic equipment, accompanied constantly by the redoubtable James McDougall, who carried Rupert's heavy cameras and other photographic gear, and generally made himself indispensable. 'McDougall has possession of papa all day long,' Beatrix noted,

> his keenness for photography is something surprising, they carry on in what ought to be the larder. There is naturally time for a great deal of conversation.

Both men were well read, 'and McDougall's stories when they begin to run short are a standing joke'.[24] In fact, the friendly local station-master Mr Kinnaird, who knew McDougall well, was according to Beatrix 'quite convulsed when papa told him how McDougall attributed the rough weather to the passage of the planet Satan over the Equator'.[25] McDougall's pronouncement was obviously thoroughly enjoyed not only by Mr Potter and Mr Kinnaird, but by Beatrix too as she recorded with ill-concealed mirth, 'It is really indecorous to make a Station-master laugh in that profane manner on the platform.'[26] McDougall, now retired, lived with his wife and daughter Maudie in the nearby hamlet of Inver, taking an interest in local affairs and looking after his bees. Old Miss Duff, sister-in-law to McDougall, also lived with the household.

As Heath Park was within easy walking distance he spent much of his time there in the Potters' company, freely dispensing his wit, wisdom and opinion on every conceivable subject. Beatrix frequently referred to him in her *Journal*

9.4 **Peaceful Inver.**

during the 1892 holiday in Birnam, writing down his many pronouncements as well as she could in imitation of his native Scots accent, the sound of which delighted and amused her in equal measure. The Potters knew James McDougall from their Dalguise years, when he had worked on the estate. Subsequently he became game-keeper there when Robert McIntosh left in 1879 after 26 years' service, to take up the post of head game-keeper to the Duchess Anne on the Atholl Estate. Many years later Beatrix referred to James McDougall as 'our old game-keeper'[27]. Now that his time was his own McDougall continued to accompany Rupert and Bertram on their fishing trips, for they valued and respected his expertise and local knowledge in the sport as much as ever. One showery day in August Beatrix herself joined her brother and McDougall for a spot of fishing on the River Braan. 'McDougall caught a good trout and lost a better. I lost a smallish one, and Bertram caught a moderate.'[28] The Potters clearly enjoyed the company of their spirited and colourful old friend and the feeling was mutual. Even on wet days McDougall could be found at Heath Park where according to Beatrix 'he consoles himself with reading the newspapers in the kitchen to the aggravation and inconvenience of the maids'. However, 'he is also great at cleaning off old negatives with *monkey* [a brand cleaner]'.[29]

Rupert Potter's interest in photography, pioneered by a Perth man, David Octavius Hill (1802–70), fascinated McDougall and caused Beatrix to remark, 'If he is once allowed to get possession of the camera, the only way to get him out of the velveteen is to invite him to pose in the picture.'[30] McDougall's admiration for Rupert Potter's considerable talent as a photographer was genuine and Rupert was pleased to share his knowledge with him. Although drawing and painting was her first love Beatrix was eager to improve her own photographic skill and was learning more all the time with guidance and encouragement from her father, in whose expertise she was justifiably proud.

> Papa brought out some very good photographs, there is one of the Cathedral which has kept McDougall awake at night. They are superior: they are better than Mackenzie's: they are as good as Wilson's of Aberdeen.[31]

Wilson had photographed The Hermitage after the folly had been restored following the Dunkeld toll bridge riots. Inside the vestibule of the restored building a picture of 'Beardie Willie' (Willie Duff), a keeper on the Atholl Estate, replaced that of Ossian, the legendary Celtic bard and warrior. A. F. Mackenzie photographed Beardie Willie, who was known to the Potters and to McDougall, clad in the working clothes worn by keepers on many Highland estates at the time. He is holding a fishing rod and wears the kilt, tweed jacket, brogues and a Tam o' Shanter, the latter garment very like the one Beatrix painted years later for little Benjamin in *The Tale of Benjamin Bunny*. The picture is now kept at Blair Castle.

A. F. Mackenzie was the local Birnam photographer who had set up his studio in Station Road in 1867 with one employee, Miss Jane Martin, who remained his assistant for 30 years, the business finally closing in 1937. A mild-mannered man with an artistic disposition and intellectual tastes, A. F. Mackenzie was interested in landscape photography, producing many views of the countryside around Dunkeld for the respected photographer George Washington Wilson of Aberdeen, who was also a personal friend. Mackenzie's best work, however, was portraiture, his most famous photographs being those of Sir John Millais and Helen Beatrix Potter. In 1892 he photographed Beatrix at his Birnam studio. She is wearing a long-sleeved dress trimmed with dark beads, the design of which

9.5 **Beatrix Potter age 26.**

Photograph by A. F. Mackenzie of Birnam.
Reproduced by kind permission
of Frederick Warne & Co.

is perhaps a little severe for her age. Her hair is worn in a simple unpretentious style, her expression is thoughtful but inscrutable.

It is interesting to note that despite the fine photographic talent of her father, on this occasion the professional services of Mackenzie were engaged instead. Although a good proportion of commissions undertaken by Mackenzie were portraits entailing detailed scrutiny of clients through the camera lens, Beatrix noted that otherwise he 'does not look you in the face'.[32]

Mr Mackenzie lived with his wife (they had no family) at nearby Birch Wood, which Beatrix described as a 'very genteel and snug little house'[33] and it was there in October 1892 that Beatrix had met, for the first time, the photographer's wife and Miss Martin. Before her marriage Mrs Mackenzie had been Annie Mackie, daughter of James Mackie, a former head gardener to the Duchess of Atholl. With her improved status in life Mrs Mackenzie had developed 'a certain air'[34] and although Beatrix found her pleasant enough, of the two women Beatrix preferred Miss Martin, whom she immediately liked and was glad to have met.

The ability to drive the pony carriage with increasing confidence gave Beatrix a new freedom. She still accompanied her parents on outings of course, particularly her mother, who enjoyed leisurely excursions in the comfort of the family's phaeton driven by their own coachman. Beatrix recalled such a drive to Ballinluig one afternoon in early August and the return journey through the beautiful woods at the foot of Craigie Barns, the steep and craggy hill, 1000ft high, just north of Dunkeld. It was the fourth Duke of Atholl, often known as the Planting Duke for the great number of trees he planted on the Atholl Estates, who solved the problem of distributing trees on such steep ground by using a cannon loaded with seeds. Not far from the crags nestles the lovely Pulney Loch, or pike pool, from the Scottish Gaelic *Polnan-Geadas*, the first in a necklace of small lochs near Dunkeld. On such a glorious summer's day as that enjoyed by Beatrix and her mother it would have been hard to imagine Pulney Loch in winter, frozen solid, a favourite place for local men to enjoy the game of curling on the ice.

Occasionally Beatrix and Bertram went together in the pony carriage, but the outings Beatrix enjoyed best were those she made alone when she could absorb the countryside as she drove. Quite often she took the camera with her. The pony carriage also made independent visiting very easy.

CHAPTER TEN

'...the mysterious good folk.' [1]

ONE OF THE FIRST people Beatrix went to see that summer of 1892 was 83-year-old Kitty MacDonald, now living at Inver but still 'waken, and delightfully merry'[2] despite her age. Kitty had expected to live out her remaining years at remote Kincraigie and as the summer of 1891 drew to a close she had begun, as usual, to gather sticks for winter fuel, storing them in the loft of her cottage where they would be dry. About this time an elderly man unexpectedly came to live next door to her and because of this Kitty decided to leave. Before departing from her cottage, however, she burnt all her hard-gathered sticks in great fires which lasted for several days rather than leave them behind. Kitty now spent her days knitting, an employment that earned her a few extra shillings: 'Mamma and I went to pay Kitty 7/6 for knitting stockings,' Beatrix recalled. 'I never saw any one so delighted with the possession of coin. She shook it up in her hand and fairly chuckled.'[3] Beatrix, who did a little hand knitting herself, was always interested in what her friend was creating. In her prime Kitty had also been expert in hand-spinning, a skill she had learned as a girl from her mother. Knowing that Beatrix was interested in this, one day she brought out a ball of wool in unbleached yellow that she had spun more than 40 years ago. Beatrix broke off a little piece of the wool for a keep-sake, which greatly amused and pleased Kitty. After some further searching a linen garment was produced which the old lady showed to Beatrix with pride, explaining that she had spun it with her own mother over 60 years back. The garment would no doubt have seen much use during those years, but the fact that it was hardly worn at all seemed to Beatrix a testament to the fine workmanship of mother and daughter. Despite her advancing years Kitty still attended church, although she admitted to Beatrix that she found it 'a long waak to the Kirk'[4], but nevertheless she was still a regular worshipper there. Dressed in black and carrying her Bible and hymn book, which she wrapped up in white paper, she was often seen on a Sunday hurrying along from Inver to the church at Little Dunkeld a mile away in time for the service.

Beatrix loved visiting Kitty, sitting at her fireside sharing the old lady's wealth of reminiscences and memories of times long ago as the logs crackled peacefully in the hearth and *sodjers* [a Scots name for small sparks of burning soot] glowed at the back of the chimney. And she admired Kitty's cheerful independence. Here

10.1 **The kirk at Little Dunkeld.**

the welcome was always warm and Beatrix returned many times before the end of the holiday.

Kitty had been born at Easter Dalguise, the youngest of eight children. Her crofter father had died soon after her birth and at the age of seven Kitty was sent to live with an uncle on his farm near Ballinloan. Here she worked as a herd up on the hill, looking after his sheep and cattle until she was 18. Although life in the hills during the summer months could sometimes be idyllic, when the ewes were milked and cheese made, more often her days were a succession of hard work. And with little time for leisure Kitty reflected, 'There was less tea drunk then.'[5]

The countryside on the Dunkeld side of Telford's bridge held much that interested Beatrix and she often chose to drive in that direction in the pony carriage. Sometimes she turned northwards from Dunkeld, following the route of General Wade's military road towards the small settlement of Guay. Here, one hot day late in August, she saw Scotland's largest game bird, 'a beautiful cock capercailzie [sic] in the top of a fir tree'.[6] Capercaillie is a Gaelic word meaning 'horse of the wood'. The journey to Guay took Beatrix past St Colm's farm where long ago ancient Rotmell Castle had once stood, now long gone. Interestingly for Beatrix, according to Donald McLeish, the game-keeper at Kinnaird, it was there that the first rabbits ever seen in the district appeared.

Another day Beatrix drove over the bridge to Calley to photograph under-keeper Charlie Lamm's captive fox. This had caught her interest following an extraordinary story Donald McLeish had related concerning a fox he had trapped in a snare as part of his work as an estate game-keeper. When he found

it, the fox was sitting upright with the wire around its neck but when he walked behind the creature to shoot it, the fox dropped to the ground first as if dead. Foxes are extraordinarily sensitive animals and especially wary of humans but, despite this, it kept up the pretence of being dead, and allowed McLeish to handle it and drop it into his game bag which he took home. The fox lived on porridge in a kennel for six years afterwards and was prevented from escaping by a chain around its neck. It also managed to catch the occasional hen by feigning sleep and then springing upon any unsuspecting fowl that wandered near its dish, where it had left, by way of bait, a small portion of porridge. In the event, Charlie Lamm was not at home and the fox was uncooperative for photographs. The strange story remained with Beatrix however and reappeared in a group of other paintings and drawings from the mid- to late 1890s which are thought to be early ideas for book illustrations. The painting titled 'The Fox and the Grapes' clearly shows a fox sitting upright upon a wooden hutch. It wears a chain collar and lead tethering it to the hutch, and the hutch itself is located in an enclosure of some kind. A short distance away lies a food dish and the fox licks his lips as he waits for his quarry, pigeons instead of hens. Beatrix also painted another study of the fox wearing a chain collar and lead and she eventually did succeed in photographing Charlie Lamm's 'foax'[7] during a return visit that autumn, when Charlie held the unwilling creature still for the camera. 'I thought every moment he would be bit,'[8] a relieved Beatrix confessed. The fox expedition was not a wasted journey. The fragrant woods at the foot of Craigie Barns, where many Scots pine trees grew to a great height, were cool and beautiful on that day of soaring temperatures. Beatrix was touched by the kindness of Mrs McIntosh, who 'let the pony stand in their stall, gave me a glass of milk, and tramped up the wood with me to the Under-keeper's cottage'.[9]

Mrs McIntosh was the wife of retired game-keeper Robert McIntosh, a man universally respected throughout the district. The McIntosh's woodland cottage 'with its bright old-fashioned flowers and a row of bee hives'[10] instinctively appealed to Beatrix, but she was puzzled by an intriguing stone structure surrounded by iron railings and filled with water which stood nearby. Mrs McIntosh explained with a shudder that this was the 'Eel Stew',[11] a holding pen for live eels caught in nearby hill lochs for the delectation of the Duchess of Atholl. Her Grace apparently enjoyed one or two of these eels cooked for her supper each evening. The explanation reminded Beatrix of her great-grandfather Abraham Crompton and his taste for live snails gathered from the garden ivy and cooked in butter and parsley for supper. She did not however share this recollection with Mrs McIntosh. The 'Eel Stew' is still there today.

During the summer months a number of annual events took place in Birnam and most of these were well attended by local people and visitors alike. In particular, Birnam Highland Games, held on 25 August 1892 (to this day the Games take place in the village on the last Saturday of August each year), saw crowds streaming into the village from far afield, many arriving by train. The weather on the previous day had been wet and there were fears that the 28th

Annual Gathering might be spoiled by even more rain. Fortunately the organiser's worst fears did not materialise and the Games were blessed by a day of beautiful sunshine, with the number of spectators attending estimated to be around 7,000. John Kinnaird, the Birnam station-master, was responsible for seeing the expected crowds heading for the Games through the station in an orderly fashion. He had been appointed by the Highland Railway Company 30 years earlier, arriving from Inverness to take up his appointment. His duties each year also included welcoming the many distinguished visitors who had summer villas in Birnam when they arrived by train.

'Mr. Kinnaird is a rather fine-looking old gentleman,' Beatrix observed,

> with a long white beard tinged with yellow, a bluff red face, tall and sprucely dressed in a station-master's blue frock-coat with brass buttons.[12]

He was a bachelor and lived with his brother James, the local coal merchant who also ran an estate agency business. Both men lived at Old Birnam Lodge where Miss McPherson, their cousin, kept house for them. Mr Kinnaird clearly took his station responsibilities very seriously, privately expressing certain anxieties to Rupert Potter beforehand about the invasion of his station on the day of the Games.

Happily, all went off smoothly. The Potters had probably attended Birnam Games many times in the past, enjoying the colour and spectacle. The skirl of the bagpipes in the open air, the feats of strength demonstrated by competitors in events such as tossing the caber and hammer throwing, along with traditional Highland dancing, were some of the attractions. Throughout her life Beatrix loved to watch country folk-dancing, although she never took part herself. Years later, as Mrs Heelis of Sawrey, she took enormous pleasure in watching her husband Willie, who was an enthusiastic exponent of local traditional dancing. But for that 1892 holiday, perhaps wishing to avoid the throng or even the wet grass from

10.3 **Station sign post in English and Gaelic.**

the previous day, the Potters decided against attending the Games. Instead they had a grandstand view of proceedings from the garden of Heath Park, 'standing on two garden benches and a buffet, all three of us, and McDougall looking over the yew hedge'.[13] There is no mention of Bertram. On other days, from the same vantage point they could also see Mr Kinnaird going about his duties 'having a bird's-eye view of the goods' yard,' as Beatrix observed,

> which he [Mr. Kinnaird] constantly crosses at a rapid shuffle, coming from his house to the station... goes fast with a rolling gait and short steps, always with his hands in his pockets.[14]

Unfortunately the unfriendly McInroys next door had the same idea of viewing the Games from their garden, blocking the Potters' view in the process. Several weeks later certain information concerning the mysterious and aloof McInroys emerged. Far from having a 'fine place and nineteen miles of deer forest' as Beatrix put it,

> the distinguished Mrs. McInroy came from Stockport, and Mr. McInroy, in spite of his kilt, is but a mushroom laird (his father bought it from the Robertsons forty years ago, which is but a grain in the hour-glass in a land where every other chieftain is descended from Fergus McFungus.[15]

As an afterthought Beatrix added, with perhaps a touch of satisfaction, that 'the kilt is rather a sign of an Englishman, or at all events town'.[16]

If the weather had been kind for Birnam Highland Games the opposite was the case for Bostock & Wombwell's Menagerie, a travelling circus that was gradually working its way round Perthshire. It would be in Dunkeld for one day only. Beatrix always found the strangeness of a circus an irresistible attraction. She somehow persuaded Bertram to go with her, on a very wet night, to see the evening performance under canvas at Dunkeld town square. Admission was one shilling, children sixpence (feeding time 9.30 p.m. threepence extra). Despite a number of curious local people outside, once inside, Beatrix and Bertram 'found there was no other audience but ourselves.'[17] The circus continued next day on what it called its 'Farewell Tour' with shows at Stanley, Couper Angus, Perth and Crieff. A circus however was no more than an occasional spectacle in a small Highland community such as Dunkeld, and relatively unimportant to inhabitants more used to making their own entertainment.

The Annual Flower Show on the other hand, like the Highland Games, *was* an important event in the local calendar and one which the Potters had always attended while on holiday in Perthshire. Although not known to be actively interested in gardening himself, Rupert Potter had been a member of the Honorary Committee of the Rose and Pansy Association. Beatrix recalled with nostalgia the crowds and the excitement of those earlier flower shows, which she felt were better. Especially memorable to her was the musical entertainment provided on the fiddle by none other than postman Charlie McIntosh and another local man 'knitting their brows and fiddling as if for dear life'.[18] Charlie had been employed at Inver sawmill and it was whilst working there in 1857, at the age of 19, that he lost the fingers and thumb of his left hand in an accident with a circular saw. As a result he was no longer able to work at the sawmill and the following year he became the local postman, at 12 shillings a week, a position he retained for the next 32 years. From boyhood Charlie had been interested in botany and owned a copy of *Ferns and their Allies* by Dr Thomas Moore, a present to him from his mother. His quest for knowledge, however, sometimes brought him into conflict with local game-keepers who objected to anyone found wandering in the woods or over the moors where they might disturb game. But Charlie disturbed nothing and quietly and calmly pursued his passion regardless.

During the years of his post round Charlie was able to observe the natural world on a daily basis as he delivered the mail and he became very knowledgeable in many aspects. Although his principal interest was always mosses and ferns, he was also formidably well informed about fungi. Of the latter he discovered 13 species new to Britain and four new to science. In 1872, 20 years before the Potters' holiday at Heath Park, Charlie had met Dr Francis Buchanan White who in 1867 had founded the Perthshire Society of Natural Science, membership of which gave access to the Society's library. Dr Buchanan White proposed him as a special Associate Member. It was a turning point in Charlie McIntosh's life. Not only could he use the library, but he now came into contact with many leading authorities in the field of natural science including Henry Coates the fungi expert, James Menzies and Thomas Meldrum, whose special interest, like Charlie's, was mosses. Before long Charlie became involved in the recently formed Cryptogamic Society of Scotland, whose members contributed specimens of ferns, lichens, liverworts and mosses, as well as fungi, to the Society's 'Fungus Shows'. One of these was held at Perth in 1875 and another, two years later, at Dunkeld. The highlight of that memorable year for Charlie was attending the meeting of the Society himself. There, as well as exhibiting specimens, he met the Reverend John Stevenson of Glamis, who was widely regarded as one of the foremost experts of the day. At the close of the meeting Charlie and his brother played the fiddle and the cello to the delight of all assembled.

Despite his disability Charlie was active in the local community, and Beatrix admired his indomitable spirit and energy. In 1892 she noted that he 'plays the violoncello, also leads the choir at Little Dunkeld; superintends the town band, and carries off the amateur prizes at the Rose and Pansy Show'.[19] Charlie was also fascinated by standing stones, cup and ring marks and other evidence of early man found in the countryside around his home. He made collections of anything he felt worth preserving, from prehistoric stone arrow-heads to implements and objects that were once commonplace in the district when he was a boy but which, with the passing of the years, were becoming less so.

In 1890, at the age of 51, Charlie had retired from his post duties on health grounds following repeated attacks of pleurisy. With his pension of 10 shillings a week, he continued to live at Inver with his mother and brother and to pursue his interests and his botanising to the full. Charlie had faithfully delivered the mail to the Potters throughout their Dalguise years and they may well have contributed to the gold watch presented to him by the inhabitants of the Dalguise postal area in 1877 in recognition of his dedicated service as their postman. It is also interesting to note that in 1887 Charlie accepted from Rupert Potter a gift of books about fungi, a subject of mystery to Rupert but not to Beatrix and Charlie. It is reasonable to suppose that Beatrix, guessing that the Reverend John Stevenson's *British Fungi (Hymenomycetes)*, newly published in two volumes would perhaps be too expensive for Charlie to afford, influenced her father into offering the books to him as a gift. The gesture was typical of Rupert's own father and Charlie's acceptance of the books pleased Rupert very much. We can certainly suppose that Beatrix was very pleased too. The books were duly wrapped up for posting, Rupert first affixing as a book-plate the Potter family crest and writing upon it the simple inscription that the books were to Charles McIntosh of Inver, Dunkeld from Rupert Potter of London. Fungi had always been plentiful in the woods and waysides around Dalguise. The locals called them *puddock-stuils* (toadstools) and regarded them with suspicion as a source of food. In his *Herbal* of 1633 Gerard regarded all fungi as 'not very wholesome meat' and advised those who risked tasting them to 'beware of licking honey among thorns'. (Years later Beatrix had her own copy of the *Herbal*, which she kept at Hill Top.) But to Beatrix toadstools were always strangely beautiful and mysterious. In 1905, in her Book of Rhymes, she even portrayed them humorously in her painting 'Toads' Tea Party' which depicts a group of six fat toads taking tea seated around a woodland table on fat toadstools.

By the autumn of 1888 the painting of fungi had begun to capture Beatrix's serious interest. Entranced by the beauty of their shape and colour, she recorded descriptions of them in her *Journal*. As yet she lacked the knowledge to name what she found either in English or Latin, describing the Common White Helvella (*Helvella crispa*) 'like a spluttered candle',[20] and noting that the Wood Hedgehog (*Hydnum repandum*) had 'white spikes on the lower side'.[21] In the latter she omitted to include a background to give valuable habitat clues. She was however determined to learn.

Beatrix was surprised to discover that Charlie McIntosh, an apparently shy man, greatly enjoyed women's company, yet despite various courtships remained a bachelor. 'Either the ladies refuse him at the crisis,' Beatrix commented privately to her *Journal*, 'or more probably he never asks them.'[22] She hoped there would be an opportunity to ask Charlie McIntosh for his opinion about the fungus paintings on which she had been working. She greatly respected his expertise in this field and knew that if a meeting could be arranged she would learn much from him. This was, however, easier said than done. Although Beatrix and the family had known Charlie for many years in his capacity as their postman, and although he seemed to be confident and popular in the company of local women, a large social gulf existed between Charlie and the Potters. 'When one met him,' Beatrix wrote in her *Journal*,

> a more scared startled scarecrow it would be difficult to imagine. Very tall and thin, stooping with a weak chest, one arm swinging and the walking-stick much too short, hanging to the stump with a loop, a long wisp of whisker blowing over either shoulder, a drip from his hat and his nose, watery eyes fixed on the puddles or anywhere, rather than any other traveller's face.[23]

Perhaps a meeting would be awkward. As each week of the holiday passed Beatrix began to wonder if she would ever manage to ask Charlie about her work, especially after one unfortunate and embarrassing chance encounter. On her way home from a drive up Strathbraan, 'we overtook that mysterious person Mr. Charles Mcintosh [sic], obstinately absorbed in the *Scotsman*. I looked sharp round directly we had passed and caught him, which was almost unkind.'[24] There was little she could do at present except continue to work on her drawings.

CHAPTER ELEVEN

'...we had several hours in Perth...
There is no impressive volume of water like the Tay,...' [1]

APART FROM THE INITIAL flurry of settling in at Heath Park the Potters were glad to be back in Perthshire. For Beatrix every precious day there was savoured to the full and recorded in her *Journal*. Even her parents, so used to the rigid self-imposed routine of their London lives, found Birnam pleasantly refreshing. The Potters also hoped that an active holiday in Scotland would curtail Bertram's drinking and Rupert had already arranged to send his son to Oxford in mid-October, thinking that new surroundings would somehow help.

Rupert Potter and McDougall made photography trips together as far away as Killin, a small village at the head of Loch Tay. For the same purpose they travelled through the great brown hills of the historic Pass of Drumochter, Beatrix going with them this time, to the remote settlement of Dalwhinnie. Unfortunately, when they arrived, no photography was possible. Thick hill mist had swept in, obscuring the glorious view down lonely Loch Ericht to the high hills of Ben Alder forest in the distance. At other times, when river conditions were right, Rupert and McDougall fished with Bertram.

Mrs Potter seemed equally invigorated with holiday energy for she and Beatrix walked part-way up Birnam Hill, from where they enjoyed wide views south over Strath Tay and northwards to Blair Atholl. Looking down towards the field in Birnam where the 700 or so Perthshire Volunteers were practising their manoeuvres, Beatrix had reflected on the tactical brilliance of the great Scottish General, the Marquis of Montrose. In these hills, long ago, with an army not much larger and in bitter winter conditions, Montrose had out-manoeuvred the professional army of David Lesley 'and finally held the whole of Scotland'.[2]

Mrs Potter was also content to go shopping in Dunkeld without Beatrix, or to make visits to old friends and acquaintances on her own. Beatrix and her mother were never really close but a more companionable atmosphere between mother and daughter is discernable in the entries Beatrix made in her *Journal* during that summer in Birnam. Perhaps the holiday in Perthshire brought a measure of fresh Highland air into their relationship. Mrs Potter sometimes visited friends at Dalguise, but on those occasions she was rarely accompanied by Beatrix who was conveniently occupied elsewhere. One day Beatrix *did* drive part of the way along the Dalguise road on her own. At the Toll Bar beside the peaceful cottages at Dalmarnock, where the road narrows and runs parallel with the railway, she paused to take in the scene. Here she decided to turn back. If she momentarily allowed her thoughts to drift back to the Dalguise days of her childhood, 'meeting the train at startling close quarters'[3] suddenly brought her back to the present.

Quite often Beatrix encountered tinkers and tramps on her drives about the district. On the narrow roads it was sometimes a tight squeeze for her pony carriage and the tinker's caravan, packed with baskets and tinware and pulled along by a cuddy [the Scots word for a donkey or horse] to pass each other. However Beatrix was always aware that she observed a scene and a way of life that was closed to outsiders. Sometimes she would recognise individuals, like an old woman encountered one day on the Stanley road 'whom I remember, not changed in the slightest during the last fifteen years'.[4] Another quite pretty girl was remembered because each summer she came round selling baskets with her blind grandmother. On another day, again driving along the Stanley road, Beatrix paused to listen to an elderly tinker man who played, with great feeling, a selection of Scottish tunes on his violoncello. When he had finished, Beatrix gave the old man an extra threepence to play again the old Scots ballad *The Flowers of the Forest*, wishing as she did so that 'I was not always short of money'.[5] Other tinkers however were tough and mean and often there were many skinny children travelling with them, 'dirty shock-headed little rascals, but as merry as grigs on a fine day'.[6]

The dimensions of Heath Park did not encourage Mrs Potter to entertain in the way she was used to when at home in London or, for that matter, in the past at Dalguise House. Nevertheless, she did invite friends, such as Mrs Culbard, the doctor's wife, to tea. Occasionally other acquaintances living locally would also call unexpectedly, Heath Park being a convenient short walk from the village. One such couple was Mr McKenzie, Minister of Little Dunkeld, and his wife. While Mrs Potter poured afternoon tea for her guests Beatrix privately recalled McDougall's humorous comment about the Minister's zeal, '"He pursues we to the death!"'[7] The couple, Beatrix noted over her teacup, were like chalk and cheese, the Minister 'a big, hearty man with a kind manner',[8] his wife 'a pleasant little person, with rather a scared air'.[9] The Minister, it seemed, frequently got himself into scrapes by taking sides, rather than remaining safely neutral, in petty parish quarrels.

The local newspaper, *The Perthshire Advertiser and Strathmore Journal* [The PA], published on a Monday, Wednesday and Friday, price one penny, included an

'Information for Visitors' column. It also included for the benefit of tourists 'Objects of Interest' to be found in the Dunkeld and Birnam area, the famous Birnam Oak for instance being noted in this second category. As well as bowling, tennis and cricket for the energetic, also available in Dunkeld was a Reading Room and Public Library and in Birnam, The Birnam Institute, brainchild in 1880 of station-master John Kinnaird.

Open daily from 8 a.m. until 10.30 p.m., on offer among other facilities at the Institute was a Reading Room and Library. The membership fee for the Institute, which remained unchanged until 1957, was 5/- for men and 3/6d for ladies and juveniles, with special rates for visitors. Back home in London the Potters already took *The PA*, which Beatrix thought 'an extraordinary paper for anecdotes from London which do not appear in the London papers'.[10] The Potters, already well aware of the visitor attractions in the Dunkeld area, were happy to pay their subscription enabling them, as visitors, to borrow books from the Institute during their holiday, and they signed the Visitors' Book. The caretakers at the time, who were also responsible for the Lending Library, were Mr Peter Grant, a former soldier now retired from the army, and his wife. The latter, as Beatrix observed, was 'a tall angular lady with a long nose, sharp black eyes and the remains of good teeth'.[11] Her husband 'the Sergeant' by comparison was a short bespectacled figure with definite views, which he aired freely on a wide range of subjects. Beatrix found him rather amusing. Alas, Mr Grant tended to buttonhole those whom he captured in conversation, and this along with his habit of peering too closely rather put people off him, including Mrs Potter. 'Mamma detests him,'[12] Beatrix confided in her *Journal*. In spite of this Beatrix still thought Mr Grant had some interesting things to say: 'I rather like to hear Mr Grant talk about "Her Majesty" as if she were a real live person to fight for.'[13]

Birnam Musical Society gave regular performances in the upstairs hall of the Institute and dances were also frequently organised there. Music for the dancing was provided by the band of Charlie McIntosh or their rivals, led by Alex Sim. The Institute was certainly a hub of the community. The Potters were among the many distinguished patrons who supported the Bazaar of Fancy and Other Work held on the 29 August to 1 September 1883 to raise funds for Birnam Institute.

Often seen about the village on foot, Beatrix had become a familiar figure in Birnam by the time the last swallow had departed and the first hint of autumn touched the trees. She was determined to photograph one tree in particular, the famous Birnam Oak. Although it was mentioned in the Birnam Hotel guide, as well as other handbooks for tourists, Beatrix needed no introduction to the great oak wood of Shakespeare's *Macbeth*.

This particular oak tree, gnarled and ancient and the last survivor of its clan,

11.2 **Birnam oak wood.**

11.3 **The Birnam Oak.**

had lived in her memory since the days of her Dalguise childhood. With the irrepressible McDougall to carry the camera, Beatrix successfully photographed the venerable tree, resplendent in its autumn glory.

McDougall told her that every 14 years the coppices were cut with groups then left to sprout to form new timber. Her *Journal* for that day captures the spring in her step. On the walk home the sight of a local farmer, very drunk, being driven in his gig by 'Hutton, one of the hotel drivers',[14] appealed to her sense of humour and light-hearted mood. Further on she met Mrs Culbard, the doctor's wife, 'a somewhat elegant, slight, elderly lady, of plaintively amiable friendliness'[15] who invited Beatrix to come back to the house with her to see Deb, her new Persian cat. To the private delight and amusement of Beatrix Mrs Culbard related, as they walked, all the local news which included 'the history of her seal-skin cloak'.[16] Beatrix stayed for tea with good currant jelly on dry bread served, she unfortunately could not help but notice, on less than clean crockery. Dr Culbard had just stirred from his afternoon nap and hearing that Beatrix had been busy with her camera produced some photographs of his own to show her, 'dissecting them in a thick voice and bumping up against me'.[17] In a delightful word sketch, Beatrix drew a memorable but affectionate picture of the shuffling Dr Culbard. 'When driving in his gig he sits with his feet straight out like a white flour-sack leant against a wall. He wears boy's shoes and striped stockings, kisses his hand if he does not happen to be smoking.'[18] It had been a most enjoyable day.

It is clear from her *Journal* entries that Beatrix enjoyed the encounters with people she knew in the village, finding conversation with them natural and easy. She was genuinely interested in their lives, perhaps because they were so very different from her own in London. There was Bessie Cleghorn, whom Beatrix had known from Dalguise days when they had both been children. Bessie had lost a leg since then and relied on crutches to get about, but despite her disability she was still cheerful, smiling and, as Beatrix recalled, impervious to the cold. Beatrix liked to visit Miss Jessie Anderson who kept a small shop in Dunkeld. She was full of anecdotes and stories and with a fascinating collection of old coins and other curios; Beatrix considered her to be a person of 'observation and intellect'[19] with shrewd and amusing views on politics and life in general. Amongst other things, Miss Anderson was interested in local legends, history and tales of the supernatural, but unfortunately she spoke in broad Scots and at such speed, often flitting from one subject to another, that sometimes Beatrix was hard pressed to follow the conversation. Despite this, she noted that there was usually a moral somewhere in the stories Miss Anderson told. Miss Culbard, the doctor's daughter, was another familiar face. In a dreadful accident eight years earlier she had fallen through the ice on Polney Loch and because of this was now very lame and obliged to walk with a stick. Beatrix liked her more each time they met, noting 'There is a certain patient reserved strength about her character.'[20] Her sense of humour also appealed to Beatrix, for it was very similar to her own. During one afternoon visit, when conversation had turned to the ridiculous names given to some flowers, Miss Culbard related an amusing story concerning an elderly Scots lady who had unfavourably compared her own garden roses with those of a flower shop. '"Sir Gordon Richardson had got the mildew,"' the distressed lady declared, '"and Mrs. George Dickson was covered with little beasties!" (meaning green flies).'[21] Other old friends such as Bella Dewar, 'freckled, merry, sensible, and a strong flavour of red hair and buttermilk',[22] called in at Heath Park to see the Potters. Bella brought with her a seasonal gift of a few hazelnuts from the trees at Dalguise for Beatrix. Beatrix was touched by the thoughtful gesture. Bella, who could make 'the best butter in the district',[23] had a zest for life that delighted Beatrix and in the end the visit lasted all day, the two friends chattering and laughing together about old times.

The weather during the late summer and early autumn of 1892 had been wetter than usual, but this had not in the least discouraged the Potters, or indeed other visitors, from enjoying their holidays in Perthshire. Regardless of the inclement weather visitor numbers were reported in The PA to be as great as ever with hotels and boarding-houses in the area full. Then, as now, tourism mattered.

Regardless of weather, Beatrix had twice driven round the beautiful Loch of the Lowes, first 'in a gale of wind'[24] and then 'in drizzling rain'[25], each time marvelling 'how partial rain is amongst the hills!'.[26] Hay-making was progressing well between Craiglush and Butterstone with not a spot of rain to threaten work in the fields, yet in nearby Birnam it was raining. McDougall often assessed the weather to come by the direction of the clouds, known locally as the carry. Even then, as if to confound all predictions, the showery and sometimes cold weather would suddenly give way to 'a lovely hot autumn day, burning sun and heavy dew on the grass in the shadows'.[27] Then it was hard to remember how dreich [a Scots word meaning dull and dreary] it had been only the day before. Such autumn days were made for the outdoors and, with the camera beside her, Beatrix was usually out and about in the pony carriage. A favourite route was up beautiful Strath Braan. One lovely day, although chilly when out of the sunshine, she stopped at the Toll Bar to try and photograph an endearing little collie pup who wriggled, put its little wet nose between its paws and then ran away. Another afternoon, with the leaves turning harvest gold, she returned once more to Strath Braan, driving past Drumour 'in beautiful mellow sunlight slanting against the hill-sides and stooks of corn'.[28] One morning which 'began with frost and white mist'[29] drew her back yet again as the mist 'gradually rolled up the slopes',[30] to reveal 'the sun blinking out over the beautiful valley amongst the hills'.[31]

The announcement by Brady's, the Perth Auctioneers, of a sale of furniture and miscellaneous items proved irresistible to Rupert Potter, who had an interest in such things. As unsettled weather had temporarily ruled out photography he and Beatrix, who shared his collector's enthusiasm, took the train to Perth that day. It was their first visit there since arriving in Birnam and Mrs Potter and Bertram had decided not to go with them. As the train passed Luncarty and Strathord, Beatrix was able to see for herself the extent of the damage done to the harvest by the recent rains. She also noted how widespread the practice of dishorning local cattle had become. To her artistic eye a naturally hornless animal such as an Aberdeen-Angus cow or 'Doddie',[32] with its massive broad head, was a noble beast. By comparison the unnatural result of dishorning Ayrshire cross-bred cattle with their narrow, high foreheads and large ears simply made the creatures, in her opinion, look foolish and reminded her of 'that ugliest of animals, the red deer hind'.[33] One day, as yet unforeseen and far away in the future, as a respected farmer Beatrix would cast her eye and her instinct for good stock over different animals, in particular the native Herdwick sheep of the English Lake District fells. For the present she was enjoying the railway journey, and was looking forward to seeing the sights of Perth despite it being a rather cold and damp day.

The visit seemed likely to be spoiled from the outset as Beatrix found that her new boots hurt her feet and to add to the misery they were soon soaked through. Fortunately her father came to the rescue, treating her to another comfortable pair, her second that year, which Beatrix clearly thought an extravagance. Lunch with Papa was at Woods restaurant. Beatrix chose 'bridies' and 'cookies',[34] traditional Scots comfort food on a cold day. A Forfar bridie, originally produced in the Angus town of Forfar, was and still is an individual savoury pie of meat and onions encased in a circle of pastry folded over and served warm. Plain glazed buns baked everywhere and known all over Scotland as 'cookies' were good to eat with her lemonade. After lunch Beatrix and her father strolled along Perth's wide cobbled streets noting the architecture and admiring the little gardens set back from the River Tay. At Perth Bridge they paused to watch the great river coming down in spate. A group of men, oblivious to the possibility of drowning themselves, were trying with hooks to fish a dead sheep from the swirling waters. They at last succeeded in their task 'but, upon consideration, launched it again with a boat-hook'.[35] Unfortunately, dead sheep carcasses were not the only effluent flowing into the Tay at Perth. Beatrix and her father were horrified to see large quantities of black liquid pouring from sewage arches into the water. In spite of the newspapers reporting the abatement of a cholera outbreak abroad the inhabitants of Perth were outraged because 'some extraneous Inspector has informed them and the world, that they are poisoning themselves with drinking the water of the Tay'.[36]

Perth has a fine museum. Situated in the middle of the town the building, with its distinctive domed rotunda, was the home of the Literary and Antiquarian Society of Perth. Beatrix and her father would almost certainly have wished to visit it, but unfortunately it was closed the day they were in Perth. There were, however, plenty of good shops to look at, 'especially the drapers',[37] with many specialising in shooting, fishing and hunting outfits. As well as deer stalker hats, hand-knitted knickerbockers and shooting hose, the shop windows displayed tweeds and Highland dress for ladies and gentlemen. One outfitter was proud to be patronised by their Royal Highnesses the Prince of Wales and the Duke of Edinburgh. If Rupert paused to look at fishing tackle in one shop window, perhaps Beatrix did likewise at another selling dresses and dress materials, mantles and millinery.

On offer at Brady's auction rooms that day was an assorted display of furniture, some of reasonable quality, coins, various items of china, 'an amazing blunder-buss'[38] and an array of swords. Some of the swords were of very good quality but the bucket-hilted broadswords, wielded perhaps for the last time in the doomed Jacobite cause at Culloden, were old and rusty. Rupert made a lot purchase of china and Beatrix bought a little bowl for a pound.

Earlier in the day Beatrix had puzzled over the large number of cows grazing on the lush meadowland of the Inch, but with the autumn livestock markets due to take place soon this would not have been so unusual a sight to local people as it was to visitors. In the end Beatrix and her father had to hurry to catch the train back to Birnam for they had stopped on their way to the station to look at the statue of Sir Walter Scott, complete with his adoring dog, which was situated in a quiet recess on the Inch. Beatrix did not like the statue, but then perhaps an interpretation in stone of one's idol by another person may never really

11.4 **Statue of Sir Walter Scott, Perth.**

succeed in getting it exactly right. At least it provided 'a favourite perching-place for doves'.[39] An old man trudging past the statue with a cartload of coal reminded Beatrix of Gow Crom in *The Fair Maid of Perth*. Coincidentally, *The PA* was serialising Sir Walter Scott's *Ivanhoe*, Chapter XLII appearing in the newspaper the following day. Perth people it seemed, like Beatrix, enjoyed Scott's novels for by October they were avidly reading *The Antiquary*, by instalments and unabridged in the pages of *The PA*.

CHAPTER TWELVE

'...the sun blinking out over the
beautiful valley amongst the hills,...' [1]

AS THE POTTERS CONTINUED their holiday in Birnam, red deer stags were bellowing challenges to each other across the now tawny hills of Perthshire. In the glens, rowan trees blazed with berries and smoke from cottage chimneys rose into the still air as the days shortened.

Of necessity, Beatrix had become proficient at negotiating the pony carriage down the steep and narrow lane leading from Heath Park to the village. This entailed guiding the Potters' normally placid but spirited black mare, used to the streets of London rather than the country roads of Perthshire, down an incline beside the Inchewan Burn and then under the railway bridge. The operation called for concentration and a tight hand on the reins. For the local children who played in the area around the burn, and whom Beatrix described as 'delightful little people',[2] this spectacle was not to be missed. One boy however, no doubt showing off in front of his friends, began a foolish and persistent 'bolting the pony'[3] game every time Beatrix drove the mare under the railway arch. Mr and Mrs Potter, concerned for Beatrix's safety, consulted the local policeman, 'a mild yellow-haired person, who carries a pair of white cotton gloves which he never puts on',[4] to see if he could put a stop to this game. The policeman tried, but without success, reporting that '"the laddies"'[5] were too quick for him to catch. In the end Beatrix took the matter into her own hands and 'a judicious application of the whip had most salutary effect'.[6] The result was a satisfactory truce and Beatrix was able to reach Birnam's good main road in safety.

The matter of safety on local roads, many of which were narrow, twisty and steep, had recently come into sharp focus. There had been a collision at nearby Ladywell involving Mr Reid the baker's cart, described by Beatrix as 'a cross between a Noah's Ark and a basket-caravan'[7] and a carriage coming down at speed from Drumour. Incredibly, and to everyone's immense relief, no-one was hurt and there was very little damage done beyond 'a spray of lentil beans and green sugar-bottle glass, and a great scatter of tin canisters'.[8] In the ensuing chaos Mr Reid's old horse had bolted as the harness broke and headed off in panic down the steep road towards home, and two passengers on board the cart 'fell off early in the proceedings'.[9] 'Sam'le'[10] the driver managed somehow to hang on to his seat as the now horseless cart careered off down the road and under the railway bridge before coming to a halt. Commenting on the accident (which as no one was injured had its humorous side) in her *Journal*, Beatrix recalled a narrow escape she'd had herself whilst driving the pony carriage. Based on 'my private experienced opinion', she wrote,

> the great point to be remembered is that a vehicle really tilts over comparatively slowly, and that instead of trying to save yourself by spreading your hands, you should twist round and throw up your feet. This theory, however, rather implies a top position. I have not the very slightest desire to try it a second time from underneath![11]

Beatrix was mindful of this experience again one day on the little hill road at the back of Cardney. The road was not flat, as she had imagined it would be, when with hopes of seeing Loch Ordie she had turned towards Riechip from Butterglen. As the road became steeper, in order to help the pony Beatrix got out of the carriage and led him by the bridle. With Loch Ordie hidden from view in the mist and the pony 'in a lather'[12] from his exertions, she decided to turn back. Despite a muddy road they had no difficulties on the return journey and the pony was 'only moderately apprehensive, the road being very soft with mud'.[13] Beatrix, on the other hand, seemed confident that there would not be another spill as they bowled along. 'It is surprising how well he has kept on his feet this year.'[14]

Sometimes Beatrix chose to drive the pony carriage past Eastwood House and along the road leading to Stenton, Caputh and Murthly. From this riverside road anglers standing out in the current fishing the Tay for salmon were a common sight, especially on the graceful bend of the river beyond Dunkeld Bridge. Here views of the River Tay were particularly fine. Perhaps because of her family's long friendship with Sir John Millais, the area from Dunkeld to Murthly was in Beatrix's mind much associated with the artist. Following the visit to Perth by Beatrix and her father a mix up at Brady's Auction rooms had resulted in the wrong china being delivered to Heath Park. To sort out the muddle Rupert Potter decided to return to Perth himself. While he was there he visited Sir John Millais who, with his wife Effie and family, was staying at Bowerswell in Perth, the home of Effie's mother. Although Beatrix liked Sir John Millais, she decided not travel to Perth with her father for the visit. From her childhood days at Dalguise and at home in London she found Sir John rather intimidating, although he had always taken a kindly interest in her painting, giving advice on how to mix her paints. Beatrix never forgot the compliment he had paid her when he said '"plenty of people can *draw*, but you and my son John have observation."'[15] He was always very outspoken, a trait the newspapers often characterised as '"his schoolboy manner"'.[16] Nevertheless, in adulthood Beatrix was not blind to the complex nature of Sir John's personality, reflecting,

I should think he is a character who will be described in some future day by biographers in puzzling contradiction, like Dr. Johnson. Some looking only at the noisy, coarse, selfish side, which I am afraid exists, and others who have received real kindness from him, will go to the other extreme.[17]

It is interesting to note that after their marriage Sir John and his wife had set up home at Annat Lodge in Perth, where they lived until 1862 when their main base became London. Annat Lodge subsequently became the home of Dr Francis Buchanan White, one of the great Scottish naturalists of the 19th century, founder in 1867, as noted earlier, of the Perthshire Society of Natural Science and the man who encouraged Beatrix's friend and mycology mentor Charlie McIntosh of Inver to become an Associate Member of the Society.

Millais, like Beatrix, adored the Perthshire countryside. Like the Potters he had, over the years, rented various houses in the area including, in 1879, Eastwood in Dunkeld. But his favourite was Birnam Hall, a house about a mile from Murthly Castle. For 10 years from 1881 he enjoyed the shooting and fishing that went with the lease and it was from there that many of his great Murthly landscapes were painted. Of these, one of the greatest, *Over the Hills and Far Away*, was painted by Millais while he was on holiday in Perthshire, possibly spending time with the Potters who were at Dalguise. The painting depicts a view up the Tay with the slopes of Craigie Barns [Craig a Barns on OS maps] and Craigvinean in the middle distance. Beyond is Dalguise, Kinnaird Hill and, across the Tay, Ballinluig, with a glimpse of Beinn a' Ghlo on the horizon. Perhaps Beatrix was an admirer of this splendid painting, its evocative title connecting her with the old days at Dalguise.

In her *Journal* Beatrix recorded a conversation Sir John had had with her father when the lease finally expired on Birnam Hall, 'that he could not bear to go near Birnam for the same reason that we felt about Dalguise, he was so distressed at having to leave Murthly'.[18]

Out of curiosity and because she was interested in architecture Beatrix probably visited Murthly Castle, for an entry in her *Journal* records a trip she made with the pony past Stenton and over the River Tay at Caputh Bridge. There is a driveway leading to the Castle just beyond the bridge. Commenting on the 'magnificent appearance'[19] of the Castle, Beatrix was also aware that it had never been occupied and that a former laird abandoned the building before it was completed.

Beatrix had discovered that, in the space of a single day, interesting expeditions into the surrounding countryside with the pony carriage could easily be combined with activities nearer to home, such as a leisurely reading of the newspapers. 'News in the *Scotsman* of Lord Tennyson's death, a truly great patriot.'[20] If the day was especially wet, although inclement weather rarely kept her indoors for long, Beatrix worked on her paintings and drawings. Her choice of subject matter often reflected the same degree of enquiry and lack of squeamishness which had been evident during her childhood days at Dalguise: 'drawing a ram's head, borrowed from Mr. Hendry the *Flesher*.' [21]

And of course, looking after her beloved pets, and especially her rabbit, Benjamin Bouncer, was always a priority. Safe from Miss Hutton's cat on his leather lead Benjamin loved his walks in the garden with Beatrix where he could sniff the fresh air and nibble assorted greenery. Benjamin also loved the peppermints and other 'sweeties'[22] given to him by Beatrix's father and McDougall and soon developed toothache and a swollen face as a consequence. Beatrix found an examination of his tiny mouth quite difficult, but concluded that none of his teeth seemed to be broken. 'This comes of peppermints and comfits. I have been quite indignant with papa and McDougall,' she wrote in exasperation in her *Journal*, '[for Benjamin] has not the sense to suck the *minties* when obtained.'[23] Although she scolded her father for encouraging Benjamin's sweet tooth, they were of the same mind when Beatrix rescued a little wild rabbit she found in the wood. It had a wire snare fast around its neck and 'Papa in his indignation pulled up the snare.'[24] The episode provoked a certain amount of jealousy in the pampered Benjamin when he smelt the fur of the wild rabbit on Beatrix's dress. His reaction amused Beatrix. 'Rabbits are creatures of warm volatile temperament but shallow and absurdly transparent,'[25] she wrote, reflecting on the character of rabbits in general and of her own dear rabbit in particular.

> It is this naturalness, one touch of nature, that I find so delightful in Mr. Benjamin Bunny, though I frankly admit his vulgarity. At one moment amiably sentimental to the verge of silliness, at the next, the upsetting of a jug or tea-cup which he immediately takes upon himself, will convert him into a demon, throwing himself on his back, scratching and spluttering. If I can lay hold of him without being bitten, within half a minute he is licking my hands as though nothing had happened. He is an abject coward, but believes in bluster, could stare our old dog out of countenance, chase a cat that has turned tail.[26]

Her affectionate summary of Benjamin was based on hours of observing, sketching and painting him. Beatrix was doubtless aware of old country superstitions relating to rabbits. Seeing a black rabbit, for example, might indicate the presence of an evil spirit and was therefore generally regarded as unlucky.

One should however also be cautious of a white rabbit, who could well be masquerading as a witch, and to be safe it was advisable to repeat the words 'white rabbits' a few times as a protective charm. Even so, this would only be effective if the words were the first uttered on the first day of each month. But it was the outdoors that drew Beatrix like a magnet. There was so much to see and do, to paint and photograph before the end of the holiday, but she knew that the pony needed to be rested. On such days, and undeterred by the weight of the heavy hand camera, Beatrix eagerly set off from Heath Park on foot in the hopes of an interesting photographic encounter.

She had observed roe deer (*Capreolus capreolus*) feeding in the woods behind the house, elusive elegant creatures with black velvety muzzles and graceful movements which, in an instant, could vanish into the trees. Would it be possible to photograph them, Beatrix wondered, or even to approach them unseen?

Then, one day to her delight a few of the deer strayed on to the quiet woodland path to graze tender ferns growing there. Although her intention had been to photograph these beautiful creatures she soon found the thrill of stalking and observing the deer at closer quarters more satisfying. As in all her encounters with the natural world she became totally absorbed in every detail. Enthralled, she noted the rich red colour of the coat of one individual in the group, the slim legs, the tiny black hooves, which, being plagued by midges, it lifted often to delicately scratch its ears which it flapped constantly. She observed that the roe deer lacked a visible tail, unlike fallow deer. As she crept forward, freezing into immobility when one of the animals lifted its head or paused from feeding to sample the air for danger, her fascination increased. She was in full view, but so long as she remained completely motionless and downwind from their sensitive sense of smell, the group was apparently unconcerned by her presence. They saw no threat in a stationary object. Two hinds wandered into the entrancing scene going 'lippity, lippity',[27] a word Beatrix would use again the following year when writing the famous picture-letter from Eastwood about Peter Rabbit to young Noel Moore. Beatrix had managed by now to get very close to the deer but 'overdid it at last', the spell was broken and they disappeared 'into the wood with a twinkle of red and white'.[28] No photographs had been taken, yet it had been an interesting and worthwhile morning. 'I often consider what an important factor the arrangement of the eyes must be in determining the amount of intellect in different animals,' Beatrix wrote, thinking of her encounter with the roe deer. Her thoughts read like a scientific paper on the subject.

If a man examines any object intently, he stares straight at it, seeing it at once, and equally (as regards scope), with both eyes, but in a considerable proportion of animals, the two spheres of sight do not overlap at all, and in certain species, such as bats and rabbits, there is an absolute gap between the two planes of vision. Such a state of affairs would be a strain upon a human intellect, and, unless animal minds are more comprehensive than ours, they must either concentrate their attention on one eye at a time, or get a very superficial impression from both, the latter is probably the case. When preoccupied with feeding, they rely on their ears. It would follow logically that those whose eyes are most sideways would rely most on their ears, an interesting subject to work out. The overlapping in human sight is say 15° + 15° out of 60°. [29]

The weight and cumbersome nature of camera equipment at that time meant that photography was still a long way from being a quick or spontaneous process should suitable subjects suddenly present themselves. Beatrix found this to be the case one morning when walking down to Birnam from Heath Park. In the middle of the village she encountered a flock of sheep rounded up into a close-packed group by collie dogs which were in charge of them. Beatrix watched, enthralled by the skill of the sheep dogs. This fascination and respect for Border collies increased and deepened through the years and lasted all her life. She was also intrigued by the quiet acceptance of the sheep to obey orders and stay put, as the collies and shepherds at last went off to find themselves breakfast. After a moment of indecision Beatrix hurried back to Heath Park, collected the camera, enlisted McDougall's help to carry it and hoped the sheep would still be there. She returned in time to photograph the scene just as the shepherds returned, shouting their commands in Gaelic to their hard-working collies. Unfortunately, the resulting photographs were a disappointment and Beatrix declared them to be the 'worst batch'[30] she had taken during the holiday.

Fortunately, there was the consolation of knowing that on a previous occasion, she had successfully photographed six handsome rams, or tups as male sheep are also known, standing on a wooden footbridge near peaceful Ballinloan. Beatrix had also noticed grouse winging their rapid way across the heathery hillside that day, hardy creatures that would soon be facing harsh winter weather on the high moors and hills. For the present their staple food of heather shoots, supplemented by blaeberries, was plentiful and as Beatrix watched them go, the beginnings of a lovely sunset cast soft light on old farm buildings nearby. Such a peaceful scene, yet old Kitty MacDonald could remember when there was a busy dye works, a tannery and a cobbler's shop in Ballinloan. But that, Kitty said, was a long time ago in the days before emigration to North America began. The glens were emptier places now. Once they had echoed to the sound of marching troops and on her way to Ballinloan Beatrix had crossed one of the many bridges built by the redcoat soldiers of General George Wade. General Wade had been appointed Commander-in-Chief in Scotland in 1724 by a Government nervous of possible Jacobite rebellion in the Highlands. Between 1725–37, over 250 miles of road had been constructed under Wade's command. All were designed to enable Government troops to move quickly through the hills to quell any threat from the Jacobite clans. Beatrix may even have read the following oft–quoted couplet:

> Had you seen these roads before they were made
> You would lift up your hands and bless General Wade.

As a child Beatrix never forgot the wonderful stories related by Grandmama Potter concerning the Jacobite Risings. And there was the link with the '45 in the form of some linen table napkins in Grandmama's possession, embroidered with the Royal Arms of Scotland. Nurse McKenzie had also told sentimental tales of Bonnie Prince Charlie that had captivated Beatrix when she was a little girl. The stories and the memory of the bittersweet Jacobite cause stayed with Beatrix as she grew up and were easily brought to mind among these lonely hills. During the holiday, Beatrix had mentioned the table napkins embroidered with Bonnie Prince Charlie's initials to Kitty but had drawn no response from the old lady, which privately amused her. 'Either Kitty is no Jacobite,' she wrote, 'or will not let on before the Englisher.'[31]

Like all keen photographers, Beatrix was always on the look-out for interesting things to photograph in the Perthshire landscape and scene, taking the camera with her in the pony carriage almost everywhere she went that holiday. It gave her special pleasure to photograph the people she visited and their pets and to share that pleasure with them. At Ballycock Farm, Easter Dalguise, she was warmly welcomed by her friends the Stewarts into the old farm kitchen with its great open log fire and the old wooden cupboard which had stood in the corner for over a century. Gaelic was still in daily use. Beatrix loved being part of the rush of activity as the family got ready for the novelty of having their pictures taken. Miss May Stewart had been busy baking scones on a girdle when Beatrix arrived, but dusted the flour from her hands and tidied her hair with a brush made from a white ptarmigan's foot mounted with silver. Mr Peter Stewart and Uncle Jack came in from working outside and with cousins and local children, collies, horses and farm animals all included in the photograph, the afternoon was one of fun, laughter and home-made scones for tea at the finish.

CHAPTER THIRTEEN

'When we discussed funguses he became quite excited
and spoke with quite poetical feeling...' [1]

IN MID-OCTOBER, in accordance with his father's wishes, Bertram departed to university in Oxford. Travelling with him, although under protest, was his pet jay, 'crammed into a little box, kicking and swearing'.[2] In the wild, jays (*Garrulus glandarius*) are restless birds, always on the move and with a harsh, rather unmelodious call. Little wonder, therefore, that 'Mamma expressed her uncharitable hope that we might have seen the last of it.'[3] Even Beatrix was forced to admit that, handsome and entertaining though the jay was, it was 'unsuitable for the house'.[4] With the jay finally installed in the travelling box, Beatrix cleaned out the cage in which Bertram had kept it at Heath Park. Typical of the autumn behaviour of the bird in the wild, where acorns form its staple food and which it gathers into a winter hoard, Beatrix found scraps of stale food and 'screws of paper hidden in corners'.[5]

Bertram, to the undoubted relief of his parents, had spent a constructive holiday in Perthshire, painting, fishing and taking the occasional drive in the pony carriage with Beatrix. The ancient Highland landscape of lonely hills and glens, purple moors fringed by dark forests and the splendours of the River Tay provided artistic inspiration for Bertram. Most of his work was painted on a grand scale, although quite often it was rather melancholy. Beatrix greatly admired her brother's paintings and hoped this interest would keep him away from the temptation of alcohol. With Uncle William Leech in mind where alcohol was concerned Beatrix worried that Bertram might go the same way: 'The best upbringing has sometimes failed in this family,' she confided to her *Journal*, 'and I am afraid that Bertram has it in him. Heaven grant it is not so.'[6] Brother and sister had always been friends and allies and on the day Bertram left for Oxford, Beatrix, perhaps a little sad that he was gone, 'went for a solitary drive in state in the Phaeton, nearly to Ballinluig'.[7]

Earlier in October Beatrix and her mother had taken the beautiful circular drive to Guay and Ballinluig, returning by Grandtully Bridge and Kinnaird. The main purpose of the journey was to visit Sarah, the Potters' former maid who 20 years earlier had left Bolton Gardens for Scotland to marry gamekeeper Duncan McDonald. The couple, now elderly, eked out a living at remote Tullypowrie, a place which Beatrix described as 'truly a habitation in the mountains of the moon' but with 'an exquisite view, closed in the distant west by the snowy point of Ben Lawers'.[8] The weather had been wet and windy and the roads muddy as Beatrix and Mrs Potter drove along. With snow already on the hills, great flocks of sheep were being brought down into the glens, 'little creatures, woolly white, freshly washed, bleating and pressing to the side of the road, where they snatch a mouthful as they pass',[9] to be sold at the October sheep-fair in Perth. As usual Beatrix admired 'the sagacity of the collies in sorting out their property'.[10] She also noted, with the instinctive eye of the acclaimed sheep breeder and farmer she would become years later in the Lake District, that as well as the small Highland hill sheep of the area there were also many cross-bred sheep that had been reared on the lower ground. These Beatrix thought were 'very ugly, having all the ungainliness of Leicesters, without much of their imposing size'.[11] Furthermore, she shrewdly suspected that the former 'will sell at the ruinous price of five and three pence apiece'.[12]

Out-of-the way Tullypowrie meant few visitors for Sarah who, in the two decades since her marriage, had never seen a relative or returned to visit them in England, and it was obvious that money was scarce. Duncan, now very deaf, earned what little money he could by doing odd jobs locally and Sarah took in the occasional lodger to help make ends meet. But the very isolation of their cottage in the hills meant that it was a lonely life, for the couple had no children. It was with delight, therefore, that Sarah welcomed her visitors from her old world. She had aged, of course, since Beatrix last saw her, but in other respects she remained unchanged, although Beatrix noticed that her voice had acquired a certain 'Scotch clip'.[13] Otherwise, however, 'the accent was English, and Lancashire at that, over the hills at the edge of the Derbyshire peak'.[14]

The autumn revealed a treasure trove of fungi that seemed to appear everywhere. Increasingly they intrigued Beatrix. She found them on the white trunks of silver birch trees and in the undergrowth when she walked to Inver to visit Kitty, among the coppery needles that lay beneath whispering larch, on windfall branches in Birnam oak wood and a host of other places. She found their strange beauty breathtaking. She had to draw and paint them, and learn more and more about them. Characteristically, she did.

She also kept on hoping that there would still be an opportunity to show her paintings to Charlie McIntosh before returning home to London. 'I have been trying all summer to speak with that learned but extremely shy man,' she wrote of Charlie in her *Journal*, with a touch of resignation, 'it seemed stupid to take home the drawings without having shown them to him.'[15]

13.1 *Leccinum scabrum.*
Brown Birch Bolete.
Painted by Beatrix Potter.

Reproduced by kind permission of Perth
Museum and Art Gallery, Perth and
Kinross Council, Scotland.

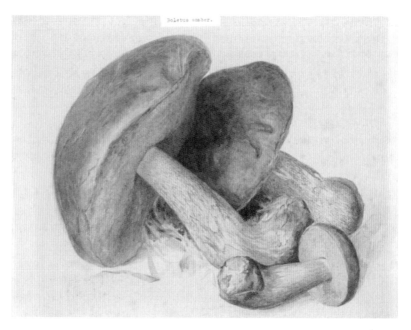

The weather had turned much colder now, with flakes of snow often in the wind and dry, withered leaves underfoot that crackled with frost. Beatrix loved the beauty of the Perthshire countryside at the approach of winter, 'the trees like fire,' she wrote, following a visit to Rumbling Bridge, 'and on the horizon a streak of pure white snow on the blue hills'.[16] In summer Rumbling Bridge was well known as a beauty spot for visitors to the area, the little stone bridge dramatically spanning spectacular waterfalls of the River Braan, and it had also become popular with artists and photographers. This was perhaps due in part to Sir John Millais' famous painting of the scene entitled *The Sound of Many Waters*, which was painted on site during November 1876, while the artist endured many discomforts of winter weather. He even resorted to working from a small hut precariously erected near the crashing waters until the work was finished. Beatrix was amused to learn from the forthright McDougall that some of the amateur artists or 'sketchers'[17] as he called them were also working from little booths sited at Rumbling Bridge. Photographers, Beatrix was also amused to learn, were similarly considered by the natives with a fair amount of contempt. Charlie Lamm (of fox fame) commented that he had even seen McDougall walking with an unnamed photographer, and Beatrix herself confessed that photographers were regarded as 'a low class'.[18] Charlie Lamm's remarks reminded her however that her own father had once been lumped into this category by mistake. The error was made at the studio of Sir John Millais one day when Rupert was photographing there. Lord Rosebery and Mr Buckle, Editor of *The Times*, were also present and in the course of conversation between these two Rupert overheard a statement he knew to be factually incorrect. 'Now, if my papa has a fault,' Beatrix wrote, 'he is rather voluble in conversation and he is oppressively well informed.' Rupert intervened and corrected Lord Rosebery who, assuming Rupert to be a common photographer, took exception and 'there was a scrimmage'.[19]

Beatrix continued to photograph whenever weather conditions allowed. She recorded the fact that there had been 12 degrees of frost one night and the following morning she awoke to find the Inchewan Burn, which had tumbled so freely to the village throughout the summer, almost stilled by ice. But the morning that accompanied the freeze was one of superb, invigorating beauty which Beatrix loved and she set off early to drive up Strath Braan in perfect weather. 'The roads were iron-bound and ringing,' she wrote, 'too dry to be slippery. In the shadows of the woods the white hoar-frost felt like a cold breath, the shadows are long now even at noon.'[20] In contrast, the hills beyond the woods basked in winter sunshine as she bowled along on quiet roads.

Once out on the uplands the sun was really hot; a cloudless blue sky and not a breath of wind. This must be the sort of bearable dry cold which they speak of in the Alps. I

13.2 **Ice on the River Braan, Perthshire.**

was surprised with the amount of ice in the Braan which gives it an oily appearance. Even in swift running water there was a bit under the shelter of every big stone.[21]

Beatrix was driving the grey pony she had used on several other photographic trips, finding his temperament ideally suited to her numerous stops and starts at various viewpoints. The obliging pony, recognising previous stopping places in Strath Braan, and perhaps like Beatrix enjoying the splendid morning, pulled up at them again. It was a day for gazing spellbound at the beauty of the quiet countryside with its blanket of snow up on the hills, but also, as Beatrix noticed, 'the snow thinly powdered was quite low-down'.[22] Before long she reached Kinloch House, situated at the head of Strath Braan where near to the road there were 'vast quantities of sheep wintering in the furrows, and a flock of grouse quite tame in the stubble'.[23] The round trip was about 15 miles and as she drove along, the cold air brushing her cheek, she absorbed the essence of the land itself and the exquisite tapestry of the country around her. As always this distillation was reflected in her drawing and painting of the creatures and plant life which fascinated her, and which inhabited a much smaller world.

At last, aided perhaps by a lucky coincidence, the meeting Beatrix had hoped for with Charlie McIntosh took place. Knowing of her interest not only in photography but also in wildlife, Mr Mackenzie the Birnam photographer had sent a rather beautiful book up to Heath Park for Beatrix to look at. To her delight the book contained 'dried ferns and moss ingeniously arranged by Charles Macintosh [sic]'[24] and this may well have provided the catalyst, or at least a proper excuse, for a meeting between the two amateur mycologists.

On a very wet afternoon in late October, Beatrix, full of excitement and not a little trepidation, arranged her fungus paintings in preparation for Charlie's visit. 'Accordingly by appointment he came, with his soft hat, a walking stick, a little bundle, and very dirty boots, at five o'clock to the minute.'[25] Charlie was evidently every bit as nervous as Beatrix. 'He was quite painfully shy and uncouth at first, as though he was trying to swallow a muffin, and rolling his eyes about and mumbling.'[26] However, Charlie quickly overcame his initial awkwardness as he began to examine Beatrix's fungus paintings, she anxiously wondering what he would think of them and what his verdict might be.

> He was certainly pleased with my drawings, and his judgement speaking to their accuracy in minute botanical points gave me infinitely more pleasure than that of critics who assume more, and know less than poor Charlie. He is a perfect dragon of erudition, and not gardener's Latin either.[27]

The ice was broken as the two enthusiasts got into their stride.

> He had not been doing much amongst the moss lately he said modestly, he was 'studying slimes', fresh water algae. I asked him to sit down, his head being somewhere in the chandelier. I would not make fun of him for worlds, but he reminded me so much of a damaged lamp post. He warmed up to his favourite subject, his comments terse and to the point, and conscientiously accurate.[28]

There was more to come as the conversation turned to fungi. 'When we discussed funguses he became quite excited and spoke with quite poetical feeling about their exquisite colours.'[29] Colour was a feature that also appealed to Beatrix and in the early stages of her study of fungi this had influenced her choice of subject for painting. She was pleased to learn from Charlie that several of her paintings portrayed rare species, two of which he had only recently found himself, these being the Common White Helvella (*Helvella crispa*) and the Wood Hedgehog (*Hydnum repandum*). The quality of Beatrix's drawings clearly impressed Charlie and, shyness forgotten in the midst of enthusiasm, he retrieved from the hall the string-tied bundle he had brought with him. This turned out to be a pocketbook containing his own detailed drawings of fungi he had found. Although the colour had faded Beatrix thought they were good nevertheless 'and as the work of a one-handed man', she noted later in her *Journal*, 'a real monument of perseverance'.[30] It is also possible that Beatrix had her own microscope to hand that important afternoon in case it might be needed. Such an instrument would have been of great interest to Charlie who did not acquire his own microscope, made by Hartnach and costing £7, until 1887. Thereafter it was in constant use and there is a photograph of Charlie with his microscope taken at home by his brother James. In the course of their meeting Beatrix told Charlie that she would soon be returning home to London and consequently there would, alas, be fewer opportunities to study fungi. Seizing the initiative Charlie offered to send fungus specimens to London by post so that she could continue to draw and study them.

He boldly suggested that if she would like to send him the drawings she made they could compare notes. It was a novel idea and although Beatrix privately wondered whether Charlie would have 'sufficient assurance to post them',[31] he evidently did. When she returned to London it seems that Beatrix made two drawings of each subject sent to her by Charlie, keeping one copy for herself and sending the other to him. During the next few years the detailed letters they exchanged about mycology show a depth of knowledge and exceptional rigour in their scientific approach. The meeting at Heath Park that October day had

13.3 **Post box at Inver. Note the 'V' and 'R; either side of the crown.**

been worthwhile, enjoyable and instructive, but most importantly Charlie McIntosh had given Beatrix scientific direction in her fungus work.

During the next few years of dedicated solitary study and experiment, Beatrix developed her knowledge of mycology to an extraordinary degree. She was encouraged in her fungus work by her uncle Sir Henry Roscoe, himself an eminent chemist who had been knighted in 1884 for his services to science. Sir Henry introduced her to the Director of Kew Gardens, Mr Thiselton-Dyer, who authorised a visitor's ticket for Beatrix, although he was somewhat surprised that any young woman should require such a thing. The ticket allowed Beatrix to visit Kew and study there, but she soon discovered that her theories and ideas were somewhat resented. She refused to be discouraged, however, by the opposition she encountered from some of the experts at Kew, much of it centred upon the fact that she was an amateur and a woman, and after long and diligent study her scientific thoroughness and persistence eventually bore fruit. Her research paper 'On the Germination of the Spores of *Agaricineae*, by Miss Helen B. Potter' was presented on 1 April 1897 to a meeting of the Linnean Society in London. As ladies were not allowed to attend the Society's meetings her paper was read by Mr George Massee FLS. After the meeting Beatrix wrote to Charlie telling him that her paper was '"well received", according to Mr Massee, but they say it requires more work in it before it is printed'.[32] It was a rather disappointing outcome.

The Potters' 1892 holiday in Perthshire, meanwhile, was almost over. For Beatrix, each wonderful month had flown past, from summer days of honeysuckle-scented hedgerows, to harvest, to Halloween. Now it was time to pack, return borrowed books to The Birnam Institute Library and begin to make farewell visits.

Beatrix would have been content to return to London without visiting Dalguise with all its past associations. Perhaps, therefore, wishing to avoid questions from Mrs Potter expressing surprise at this, or worse still her mother insisting on making a visit there with her, Beatrix 'as a duty'[33] had gone to Dalguise alone. It had been good to see the Cleghorns, the Geddeses and Mrs McLaren again. And old Miss Malloch had given Beatrix a bunch of her pansies as she had always done in the old Dalguise days.

Rupert Potter's photographic equipment and fishing rods were safely packed and, under the careful supervision of Mr Kinnaird, all non-essential luggage was already on its way to London, together with the Potters' own carriage and horses. They had all enjoyed their holiday, despite the restrictions of size afforded by Heath Park, and there was always the possibility that Rupert might consider a return to the area for next year's holiday, provided a larger, more suitable house could be found.

The recent cold and frosty weather had given way to rain that had washed footpaths away and clogged ditches with dead leaves. Most of the seasonal visitors had departed and a now quiet Birnam and Dunkeld prepared for winter. Before they left, using a hired coach Beatrix and Mrs Potter did some last-minute shopping in Dunkeld and then travelled on to Inver to say goodbye to the McDougalls, Miss Duff and Kitty MacDonald. Throughout the holiday Beatrix had been a frequent and welcome visitor to the McDougall household, often calling to buy honey from Mrs McDougall or sometimes for a chat on her way to visit Kitty. On one occasion, probably as a result of hints from McDougall himself, Beatrix had brought her camera to photograph Maudie seated at Miss Duff's spinning wheel. With McDougall's usual genius for humorous timing, laughter had overtaken the proceedings when McDougall declared the pretty setting to be '"a fraad"'.[34] Maudie was no spinner. As everyone knew, it was old Miss Duff who in her prime could spin 'like lightning'[35] and produce work of such fineness that it could be drawn through a wedding ring.

On this parting visit, Mrs McDougall had a cold and Miss Duff was a little subdued. McDougall himself, who all summer had exchanged banter with Beatrix and made her laugh so much, was now close to tears, but he cheered up a little when Beatrix presented him with a gift of a few old negatives and some printing paper. He had learned much about photography from Rupert Potter during the past months and soon recovered his sense of humour. There was one other person to whom Beatrix especially wished to say goodbye. Standing beside Miss Duff, but only reaching the height of her shoulder, was old Kitty MacDonald. Kitty, wearing a large apron and 'with quite a mountain of petti-coats up the back of her',[36] had come to help out until Mrs McDougall felt better. With her wrinkled brown hands, her twinkling eyes and her homely kindness, Beatrix was always to remember her dear old friend Kitty who had so often greeted her with the words '"I was yearnin to see ye".'[37]

Making her way on foot up the brae to Heath Park from the village for the last time on a morning returned to 'beautiful clear white frost',[38] Beatrix noticed a dipper (Cinclus cinclus) busily going about its business among the boulders and the tumbling waters of the Inchewan Burn. She paused to watch the little bird as it bobbed and dived and skimmed the surface, eventually finding a tasty morsel. But as she turned to go, Beatrix stored away the memory of its song along with so many other indelible memories of Perthshire.

CHAPTER FOURTEEN

'…so I shall tell you a story about four little rabbits whose names were –
Flopsy, Mopsy, Cottontail and Peter.' [1]

14.1 **A painting from *The Tale of Peter Rabbit* by Beatrix Potter.**

Reproduced by kind permission of Frederick Warne & Co.

THE POTTERS RETURNED TO Perthshire the following year, 1893, for their long summer holiday. This time Rupert had no anxieties about the suitability of the house he had rented: Eastwood, a spacious dower house he had leased on the Atholl Estate. Beautifully situated on the banks of the River Tay with large, well-kept gardens and a most convenient distance from Dunkeld, he was confident that the house would be entirely satisfactory. The fact that his close friend Sir John Millais had happily rented Eastwood in 1879 perhaps contributed to Rupert's confidence. He and Sir John shared similar views as to what constituted a proper holiday home. Mr Kinnaird the station-master, with the benefit of local knowledge, may also have mentioned Eastwood to Rupert as a possible let, during one of their conversations. And perhaps Rupert had already admired Eastwood for himself whilst strolling with the family through Birnam oak wood, from where the house can be seen across the River Tay.

Despite a determined New Year's resolution by Beatrix to keep a diary for 1893, the entries in it cease at the end of April that year. Unless new information comes to light in the future we shall never know her impressions of Eastwood. One thing we *do* know for certain is that on 4 September 1893 Beatrix wrote a picture-letter from Eastwood about a naughty rabbit to five-year-old Noel Moore, the son of her former governess, who had been ill. The letter began,

14.2 **Eastwood, Dunkeld.**

My dear Noel,

I don't know what to write to you, so I shall tell you a story about four little rabbits whose names were – Flopsy, Mopsy, Cottontail and Peter.'[2]

The letter was to become one of the most famous rabbit stories ever written. As it happened, the name of the tenant who had sub-let Eastwood to Rupert Potter was MacGregor. The Peter Rabbit picture-letter that Beatrix wrote to Noel Moore was, therefore, truly written in Mr MacGregor's garden! Little did Beatrix know then that *The Tale of Peter Rabbit*, as it became, together with the other 'little books' for children that followed it, would make her a household name.

The Eastwood garden gently sloped down to the edge of the River Tay and also extended for quite some distance along the riverbank on either side of the house. It was just the sort of garden that would be irresistible to wild rabbits living in the scattered woodlands nearby. Years later when Beatrix was looking for a publisher for *The Tale of Peter Rabbit and Mr. McGregor's Garden*, a friend of the Potter family, Canon Hardwicke Rawnsley, offered to help her in the task. The publication of his own book *Moral Rhymes for the Young* had brought him contacts in the publishing world. It occurred to him that success might be achieved if Peter Rabbit was presented to prospective publishers in verse rather than prose, so he set about the task himself. In discussions about the matter with Beatrix at this time it seems that Canon Rawnsley formed the impression that Mr McGregor was not only a Scots gardener but a Gaelic-speaking one at that, for he duly incorporated this information into his rhyming composition of Peter Rabbit.

Now Mr McGregor
was down on his knees
Hard at work planting cabbage
between his green peas
Up he jumped and he ran
and no dog could be fleeter
And furious he waved his rake
went for Peter;
And tho' Peter was flurried
It is his belief
That Mr McGregor in Gaelic
kept calling 'stop thief'[3]

Eastwood's garden on the banks of the Tay also contained other wildlife that fascinated Beatrix. On 5 September 1893, the day after she had written to Noel, and so that he would not feel left out, Beatrix wrote another picture-letter to Eric, Noel's younger brother, about a frog called Mr Jeremy Fisher.

14.3 **The Peter Rabbit picture letter to Noel Moore written in Perthshire by Beatrix Potter.**

Reproduced by kind permission of Frederick Warne & Co.

Eastwood Dunkeld
Sep 4 93

My dear Noel,

I don't know what to write to you, so I shall tell you a story about four little rabbits. whose names were—

Flopsy, Mopsy Cottontail

and Peter

They lived with their mother in a sand bank under the root of a big fir tree.

14.4 *Strobilomyces strobilaceus*. **Old Man of the Woods, painted by Beatrix Potter.**

Reproduced by kind permission of Perth Museum and Art Gallery, Perth and Kinross Council, Scotland.

The Moore children kept the precious picture-letters that Beatrix had sent them for years. In November 1902, a few weeks after Frederick Warne had published *The Tale of Peter Rabbit*, (they had chosen Beatrix's prose version), Beatrix wrote to Norman Warne, 'I should like to do Mr. Jeremy Fisher too some day, and I think I could make something of him.'[4]

Beatrix was still fully absorbed in her fungus studies during the 1893 holiday in Perthshire. Charlie McIntosh had been as good as his word, regularly sending fungus specimens by post to Bolton Gardens. Beatrix in turn sent Charlie paintings of them, which he carefully kept. Their correspondence had added much to her growing knowledge on the subject. On 3 September 1893, the day before she wrote the famous picture-letter to Noel Moore, Beatrix had been busy painting *Strobilomyces strobilaceus* (now *Strobilomyces floccopus*), a very rare fungus in Scotland. The common name of this fungus is The Old Man of the Woods, and Beatrix had found it in the grounds of Eastwood House.

The excitement of such a prize find was probably shared with Charlie McIntosh, for he was the only person who could appreciate and understand the significance of her discovery.

Beatrix continued her fungus forays at Eastwood, happily absorbed in drawing and painting her finds and always wanting to learn more. Importantly she was spending an enjoyable active holiday filled with nature study and painting, where she wanted to be, back in the wonderful clear air and beautiful country-side of the Perthshire that she loved.

EPILOGUE

'...an exquisite view, closed in the distant west
by the snowy point of Ben Lawers.' [1]

The Tale of Peter Rabbit, published on 2 October 1902 by Frederick Warne, changed her life and made the name of Beatrix Potter famous ever after. Beatrix did 'make something of'[2] her frog story, for in 1906 Warne published *The Tale of Mr. Jeremy Fisher*, number seven in the series of 23 of her little books to be published by them.

Charlie McIntosh continued to study fungi, to pursue his other hobbies and to donate from time to time his various collections to Perth Museum and Art Gallery. His interest in natural history remained with him for the rest of his life and he died peacefully at Dunkeld on 5 January 1922, aged 82. Charlie had been a well-known and popular figure locally and in due course a memorial was erected by public subscription in his memory. 'He was a keen observer and first-rate field naturalist 50 years ago,' Beatrix wrote of him after his death,

> and the kind of student who would continue to learn throughout a long life. It is very fitting that his name and example should be remembered and honoured in his native place. The only lasting peacefulness is Nature, and it would be well if children – old and young – would study it like Charlie Mcintosh[sic].[3]

It was in Perthshire that Bertram at last found happiness. When his brief but unhappy time in Oxford ended in failure he returned home again, but found life under the watchful eye of his parents increasingly unbearable. Sketching trips to the north of England and Scotland provided a legitimate excuse to escape from the claustrophobia of living at Bolton Gardens. On one of his sketching trips to Birnam, Bertram met Mary Scott, who was also staying in the village at the time. They fell in love and married in Edinburgh on 20 November 1902, without the knowledge of his parents. After his marriage Bertram abandoned the life of an artist to become a farmer. The couple settled happily in the village of Ancrum, not far away from Hawick, Mary's native town in the Scottish Borders. The Potters eventually discovered that they had a daughter-in-law 11 years later.

Beatrix had become a successful author and illustrator of her own work. In time she was to become a highly respected farmer and a passionate land conservationist.

In 1978, at Perth Museum and Art Gallery, the artist of a group of quality but previously unattributed watercolour paintings of fungi was identified: Helen Beatrix Potter. The discovery followed careful detective work by the late Dr Mary Noble, the distinguished plant pathologist and mycologist, and Member of The Beatrix Potter Society. Sales of the little books continue unabated and have been translated into more than 35 languages. In 2004, *The Tale of Peter Rabbit* was published in Scots for the first time. Translated by Lynne McGeachie, *The Tale o Peter Kinnen* was inspired by Beatrix Potter's love of Perthshire, the place where it all began. By happy coincidence The Beatrix Potter Society held its 11th International Study Conference in July 2004 in Perthshire at The Birnam Institute. From there, on a beautiful summer evening, with swifts carving the air around the Institute, I gave the first public reading of *The Tale o Peter Kinnen* and expressed to the Conference the hope that Beatrix would have enjoyed her famous story told in Scots.

> Aince upon a time there
> wis fower wee Kinnen, an
> thair nems wis –
> Flopsy,
> Mopsy,
> Cotton-bun,
> an Peter.
> They bid wi thair Mither in
> a san-baunk, aneath the ruit o a
> muckle fir-tree.[4]

That first vision of the Perthshire countryside, revealed to 'a little girl in a print frock and striped stockings'[5] long ago at Dalguise, never dimmed. It awakened in Beatrix a deep and abiding love of nature that burned steadily and brightly and influenced her entire life.

REFERENCES

'SO I SHALL TELL YOU A
STORY'

1   Letter to Noel Moore,
    4 September 1893.
    Frederick Warne.

INTRODUCTION

1   The Horn Book, Inc.

CHAPTER ONE

1   Linder, Leslie (ed.),
    The Journal of Beatrix
    Potter, London:
    Frederick Warne,
    new edition 1989,
    p.295
2   The Horn Book, Inc.
3   Ibid.
4   Ibid.
5   Linder, Leslie (ed.),
    The Journal of Beatrix
    Potter, London:
    Frederick Warne,
    new edition 1989,
    p.365
6   Ibid. p.47
7   Ibid. p.57
8   Ibid. p.56
9   Ibid. p.58
10 Ibid. p.56

CHAPTER TWO

1   Linder, Leslie (ed.),
    The Journal of Beatrix
    Potter, London:
    Frederick Warne,
    new edition 1989,
    p.88

2   Ibid. p.12
3   Ibid. p.219
4   V & A
5   Linder, Leslie (ed),
    The Journal of Beatrix
    Potter, London:
    Frederick Warne,
    new edition 1989,
    p.88
6   Ibid. p.88
7   Ibid. p.88
8   Ibid. p.246
9   Ibid. p.246
10 Ibid. p.246
11 Ibid. p.246
12 Ibid. p.247

CHAPTER THREE

1   Linder, Leslie (ed.),
    The Journal of Beatrix
    Potter, London:
    Frederick Warne,
    new edition 1989,
    p.10
2   Ibid. p.266
3   Ibid. p.266
4   Ibid. p.266
5   Ibid. p.266
6   Ibid. p.266
7   Ibid. p.266
8   Ibid. p.307
9a Ibid. p.10
9b Ibid. p.300
10 Ibid. p.273
11 Ibid. p.273
12 Ibid. p.267
13 Ibid. p.267
14 The Horn Book, Inc.

15 Linder, Leslie (ed.),
    The Journal of Beatrix
    Potter, London:
    Frederick Warne,
    new edition 1989,
    p.85
16 Ibid. p.94

CHAPTER FOUR

1   Linder, Leslie (ed.),
    The Journal of Beatrix
    Potter, London:
    Frederick Warne,
    new edition 1989,
    p.273
2   V & A, Drawing book
    p.9
3   Ibid.
4   Linder, Leslie (ed.),
    The Journal of Beatrix
    Potter, London:
    Frederick Warne,
    new edition 1989,
    p.93
5a The Horn Book, Inc.
5b The Horn Book, Inc.
6   Linder, Leslie (ed.),
    The Journal of Beatrix
    Potter, London:
    Frederick Warne,
    new edition 1989,
    p.93
7   V & A
8   Linder, Leslie (ed.),
    The Journal of Beatrix
    Potter, London:
    Frederick Warne,
    new edition 1989,
    p.66

9   Ibid. p.67
10   Ibid. p.215–16
11   Ibid. p.279
12   Lane, Margaret,
     The Tale of Beatrix
     Potter, Fontana Books
     1970 p. 35 (first
     published by
     Frederick Warne,
     London, 1968)

CHAPTER FIVE

1   Linder, Leslie (ed.),
     The Journal of Beatrix
     Potter, London:
     Frederick Warne,
     new edition 1989,
     p.85
2   Ibid. p.51
3   Ibid. p.291
4   Ibid. p.291
5   Ibid. p.256
6   Ibid. p.277
7   V & A October 1886
8   Linder, Leslie (ed.),
     The Journal of Beatrix
     Potter, London:
     Frederick Warne,
     new edition 1989,
     p.260
9   Ibid. p.48
10   Lane, Margaret,
     The Tale of Beatrix Potter,
     London: Frederick
     Warne, revised edition
     1968. London: Fontana
     Books 1970, p.33
11   Ibid. p.33
12   Ibid. p.33

CHAPTER SIX

1   Linder, Leslie (ed.),
     The Journal of Beatrix
     Potter, London:
     Frederick Warne,
     new edition 1989,
     p.215
2   Ibid. p.21
3   Ibid. p.305
4   Ibid. p.291
5   Ibid. p.429
6   Lane, Margaret, The
     Tale of Beatrix Potter,
     London: Frederick
     Warne, revised edition
     1968. London: Fontana
     Books, 1970, p.34
7   Ibid. p.34
8   Ibid. pp.34–5
9   Linder, Leslie (ed.),
     The Journal of Beatrix
     Potter, London:
     Frederick Warne,
     new edition 1989,
     p.307
10   Lane, Margaret, The
     Tale of Beatrix Potter,
     London: Frederick
     Warne, revised edition
     1968. London: Fontana
     Books, 1970, p.35

CHAPTER SEVEN

1   Linder, Leslie (ed.),
     The Journal of Beatrix
     Potter, London:
     Frederick Warne,
     new edition 1989,
     p.85
2   Ibid. p.261

3   Ibid. p.250
4   Ibid. p.250
5   Ibid. p.294
6   Ibid. p.294
7   Ibid. p.294
8   Ibid. p.294
9   Ibid. p.294
10   Ibid. p.295
11   Ibid. p.306
12   Ibid. p.306
13   Letter to Henry Coates
     of Perth – biographer
     of Charles McIntosh
     A Perthshire Naturalist,
     London: Frederick
     Warne, pp.123–4.
14   Linder, Leslie (ed.),
     The Journal of Beatrix
     Potter, London:
     Frederick Warne,
     new edition 1989,
     p.306
15   Ibid. p.85
16   Ibid. p.15
17   Ibid. p.16
18   Ibid. p.20
19   Ibid. pp.84–5

CHAPTER EIGHT

1   Linder, Leslie (ed.),
     The Journal of Beatrix
     Potter, London:
     Frederick Warne,
     new edition 1989,
     p.89
2   Ibid. p.39
3   Ibid. p.39–40
4   Ibid. p.87
5   Ibid. p.87
6   Ibid. p.89

7   Ibid. p.89

8   Ibid. p.89

9   Ibid. p.89

10 Ibid. p.89

11 Ibid. p.104

12 Ibid. p.202

13 Ibid. p.93

14 Ibid. p.93

15 Ibid. p.94

16 Ibid. p.92

17 Ibid. p.106

18 Ibid. p.104

19 Ibid. p.145

20 Ibid. p.201

21 Ibid. p.201

22 Ibid. p.203

23 Ibid. p.207

24 Ibid. p.208

25 Ibid. p.208

26 Ibid. p.208

27 Ibid. p.209

28 Ibid. p.213

29 Ibid. p.217

30 Ibid. p.217

CHAPTER NINE

1   Linder, Leslie (ed.), *The Journal of Beatrix Potter*, London: Frederick Warne, new edition 1989, p.248

2   Ibid. p.246

3   Ibid. p.246

4   Ibid. p.246

5   Ibid. p.246

6   Ibid. p.246

7   Ibid. p.248

8   Ibid. p.248

9   Ibid. p.247

10 Ibid. p.248

11 Ibid. p.248

12 Ibid. p.248

13 Ibid. p.274

14 Ibid. p.249

15 Ibid. p.259

16 Ibid. p.259

17 Ibid. p.259

18 Ibid. p.259

19 Ibid. p.248

20 Ibid. p.249

21 Ibid. p.249

22 Ibid. p.307

23 Ibid. p.281

24 Ibid. p.251

25 Ibid. p.298

26 Ibid. p.298

27 Ibid. p.251

28 Ibid. p.254

29 Ibid. p.280

30 Ibid. p.296

31 Ibid. p.258

32 Ibid. p.309

33 Ibid. p.308

34 Ibid. p.309

CHAPTER TEN

1   Linder, Leslie (ed.), *The Journal of Beatrix Potter*, London: Frederick Warne, new edition 1989, p.85

2   Ibid. p.250

3   Ibid. p.251

4   Ibid. p.261

5   Ibid, p.282

6   Ibid. p.257

7   Ibid. p.285

8   Ibid. p.285

9   Ibid. p.257

10 Ibid. p.257

11 Ibid. p.257

12 Ibid. p.298

13 Ibid. p.259

14 Ibid. p.298

15 Ibid. p.297

16 Ibid. p.297

17 Linder, Leslie (ed.), *The Journal of Beatrix Potter*, London: Frederick Warne, new edition 1989, p.252

18 Ibid. p.256

19 Ibid. p.306

20 Ibid. p.305

21 Ibid. p.305

22 Ibid. p.306

23 Ibid. p.306

24 Ibid. p.301

CHAPTER ELEVEN

1   Linder, Leslie (ed.), *The Journal of Beatrix Potter*, London: Frederick Warne, new edition 1989, p.247 and p.328

2   Ibid. p.249

3   Ibid. p.260

4   Ibid. p.255

5   Ibid. p.260

6   Ibid. p.255

7   Ibid. p.254

8   Ibid. p.254

9   Ibid. p.254

10 Ibid. p.71

11 Ibid. p.308

12 Ibid. p.264

13 Ibid. p.308
14 Ibid. p.296
15 Ibid. p.251
16 Ibid. p.296
17 Ibid. p.296
18 Ibid. p.296
19 Ibid. p.286
20 Ibid. p.271
21 Ibid. p.252
22 Ibid. p.270
23 Ibid. p.272
24 Ibid. p.261
25 Ibid. p.266
26 Ibid. pp.261–2
27 Ibid. p.262
28 Ibid. p.273
29 Ibid. p.273
30 Ibid. p.273
31 Ibid. p.273
32 Ibid. p.267
33 Ibid. p.267
34 Ibid. p.268
35 Ibid. p.268
36 Ibid. p.269
37 Ibid. p.268
38 Ibid. p.269
39 Ibid. p.270

CHAPTER TWELVE

1   Linder, Leslie (ed.),
    The Journal of Beatrix
    Potter, London:
    Frederick Warne,
    new edition 1989,
    p.273
2   Ibid. p.264
3   Ibid. p.264
4   Ibid. p.264
5   Ibid. p.264
6   Ibid. p.264

7   Ibid. p.264
8   Ibid. p.263
9   Ibid. p.264
10 Ibid. p.263
11 Ibid. p.263
12 Ibid. p.274
13 Ibid. p.274
14 Ibid. p.274
15 Ibid. p.429
16 Ibid. p.429
17 Ibid. p.270
18 Ibid. p.270
19 Ibid. p.253
20 Ibid. p.284
21 Ibid. p.273
22 Ibid. p.251
23 Ibid. p.277
24 Ibid. p.307
25 Ibid. p.307
26 Ibid. p.307
27 Ibid. p.276
28 Ibid. p.277
29 Ibid. p.277
30 Ibid. p.292
31 Ibid. p.282

CHAPTER THIRTEEN

1   Linder, Leslie (ed.),
    The Journal of Beatrix
    Potter, London:
    Frederick Warne,
    new edition 1989,
    p.305
2   Ibid. p.291
3   Ibid. p.291
4   Ibid. p.291
5   Ibid. p.291
6   Ibid. p.96
7   Ibid. p.291
8   Ibid. p.279

9   Ibid. p.278
10 Ibid. p.278
11 Ibid. p.278
12 Ibid. p.278
13 Ibid. p.279
14 Ibid. p.279
15 Ibid. p.305
16 Ibid. p.293
17 Ibid. p.291
18 Ibid. p.289
19 Ibid. p.289
20 Ibid. p.300–01
21 Ibid. p.301
22 Ibid. p.301
23 Ibid. p.301
24 Ibid. p.305
25 Ibid. p.305
26 Ibid. p.305
27 Ibid. p.305
28 Ibid. p.305
29 Ibid. p.305
30 Ibid. p.305
31 Ibid. p.305
32 Letter from Beatrix
    Potter to Charles
    McIntosh, 21
    September 1897.
    London: Frederick
    Warne.
33 Linder, Leslie (ed.),
    The Journal of Beatrix
    Potter, London:
    Frederick Warne,
    new edition 1989,
    p.290
34 Ibid. p.297
35 Ibid. p.297
36 Ibid. p.303
37 Ibid. p.281
38 Ibid. p.307

CHAPTER FOURTEEN

1   Letter from Beatrix
    Potter to Noel Moore
    on 4 September 1893.
    London: Frederick
    Warne.
2   Frederick Warne /
    V & A
3   Beatrix Potter &
    Canon Hardwicke
    Rawnsley, *Peter
    Rabbit's Other Tale*,
    The Beatrix Potter
    Society, London: 1989.
    Original material held
    in the V & A
4   Frederick Warne

EPILOGUE

1   Linder, Leslie (ed.),
    *The Journal of Beatrix
    Potter*, London:
    Frederick Warne,
    new edition 1989,
    p.279
2   Letter from Beatrix
    Potter to Norman
    Warne on 6 November
    1902
3   Letter from Beatrix
    Potter to Henry
    Coates. *A Perthshire
    Naturalist*, London:
    Frederick Warne,
    p.124

4   McGeachie, Lynne,
    The Tale o Peter Kinnen,
    The Beatrix Potter
    Society, London 2004,
    p.7
5   Linder, Leslie (ed.),
    *The Journal of Beatrix
    Potter*, London:
    Frederick Warne,
    new edition 1989,
    p.93

FURTHER READING

COX, EILEEN (ed.): *Dunkeld Remembered*, Perthshire: The Dunkeld & Birnam Historical Society, 1993.

EGGELING, W. J.: *Millais and Dunkeld The Story of Millais' Landscapes*, Perthshire: Dunkeld and Birnam Historical Society, second edition 1994.

HOBBS, ANNE STEVENSON: *Beatrix Potter's Art*, London: Frederick Warne, 1989.

JACKSON, HELEN M.: *A Century of Pleasures Pastimes and Service*, Perthshire: The Birnam Institute, Perthshire.

JAY, EILEEN, NOBLE, MARY AND HOBBS, ANNE STEVENSON: *A Victorian Naturalist*, London: Frederick Warne, 1992.

LANE, MARGARET: *The Magic Years of Beatrix Potter*, London: Frederick Warne, 1978.

LANE, MARGARET: *The Tale of Beatrix Potter*, London: Frederick Warne, revised edition 1968, Collins Fontana Books, 1970.

LINDER, LESLIE: *The Art of Beatrix Potter*, London: Frederick Warne, 1955; revised edition, 1972; second reprint 1976.

LINDER, LESLIE: *A History of the Writings of Beatrix Potter*, London: Frederick Warne, 1971; second edition, 1971.

LINDER, LESLIE: *The Journal of Beatrix Potter 1881–1897*, London: Frederick Warne, 1966; revised edition, 1989.

MCGEACHIE, LYNNE: *The Tale o Peter Kinnen*, London: The Beatrix Potter Society, 2004.

NOBLE, MARY: *Beatrix Potter Studies I; Beatrix Potter and her Funguses*, London: The Beatrix Potter Society, Papers presented at The Beatrix Potter Society Study Conference, 1984.

NOBLE, MARY: *Beatrix Potter Studies III, Scotland and Perthshire in the Nineteenth Century*, London: The Beatrix Potter Society, Papers presented at The Beatrix Potter Society Conference, 1988.

POTTER, BEATRIX and RAWNSLEY, HARDWICKE: *Peter Rabbit's Other Tale*, London: The Beatrix Potter Society, 1989.

TAYLOR, JUDY: *Beatrix Potter: Artist, Storyteller and Countrywoman*, London: Frederick Warne, 1986, new edition 1996 reprinted with revisions 2002.

TAYLOR, JUDY: *Beatrix Potter Studies III, The Potters on Holiday*, London: The Beatrix Potter Society, Papers presented at The Beatrix Potter Society Conference, 1988.

TAYLOR, JUDY (ed.): *Beatrix Potter's Letters*, London: Frederick Warne, 1989.

TAYLOR, JUDY (ed.): *Letters to Children from Beatrix Potter*, London: Frederick Warne, 1992.

TAYLOR, JUDY, WHALLEY, IRENE, HOBBS, ANNE STEVENSON and BATTRICK, ELIZABETH: *Beatrix Potter 1866–1943: The Artist and Her World*, London: Frederick Warne and The National Trust, 1987; Reissued 1995.

TAYLOR, LIZ: *Beatrix Potter Studies II; Bertram Potter and the Scottish Borders*, London: The Beatrix Potter Society, Papers presented at The Beatrix Potter Society Conference, 1986.

TAYLOR, M. A. and RODGER, R. H.: *A Fascinating Acquaintance*, Perth: Perth Museum and Art Gallery, 1989, updated 1995.

TAYLOR, MICHAEL A.: *Beatrix Potter Studies III; Beatrix Potter and Perthshire Natural History*, London: The Beatrix Potter Society, Papers presented at The Beatrix Potter Society Conference, 1988.

INDEX

Luath Press Limited

committed to publishing well written books worth reading

LUATH PRESS takes its name from Robert Burns, whose little collie Luath (*Gael.,*
swift or nimble) tripped up Jean Armour at a wedding and gave him the chance to
speak to the woman who was to be his wife and the abiding love of his
life. Burns called one of 'The Twa Dogs' Luath after Cuchullin's
hunting dog in Ossian's *Fingal*. Luath Press was established
in 1981 in the heart of Burns country, and now resides
a few steps up the road from Burns' first lodgings on
Edinburgh's Royal Mile. Luath offers you distinctive
writing with a hint of unexpected pleasures.

Most bookshops in the UK, the US, Canada, Australia,
New Zealand and parts of Europe either carry our
books in stock or can order them for you. To order
direct from us, please send a £sterling cheque, postal order,
international money order or your credit card details (number,
address of cardholder and expiry date) to us at the address below.
Please add post and packing as follows: UK – £1.00 per delivery
address; overseas surface mail – £2.50 per delivery address;
overseas airmail – £3.50 for the first book to each delivery
address, plus £1.00 for each additional book by airmail to the same address. If your
order is a gift, we will happily enclose your card or message at no extra charge.

Luath Press Limited
543/2 Castlehill
The Royal Mile
Edinburgh EH1 2ND
Scotland
Telephone: 0131 225 4326 (24 hours)
Fax: 0131 225 4324
email: sales@luath.co.uk
Website: www.luath.co.uk

ILLUSTRATION: IAN KELLAS